☆ A BROOKLANDS ☆
'ROAD TEST' LIMITED EDITION

WESTFIELD

Compiled by
R.M.Clarke

ISBN 1 85520 3758

 BROOKLANDS BOOKS LTD.
P.O. BOX 146, COBHAM,
SURREY, KT11 1LG. UK

A-WESX1

Brooklands Books

MOTORING

BROOKLANDS ROAD TEST SERIES

Abarth Gold Portfolio 1950-1971
AC Ace & Aceca 1953-1983
Alfa Romeo Giulietta Gold Portfolio 1954-1965
Alfa Romeo Giulia Berlinas 1962-1976
Alfa Romeo Giulia Coupés 1963-1976
Alfa Romeo Giulia Coupés Gold Port. 1963-1976
Alfa Romeo Spider 1966-1990
Alfa Romeo Spider Gold Portfolio 1966-1991
Alfa Romeo Alfasud 1972-1984
Alfa Romeo Alfetta Gold Portfolio 1972-1987
Alfa Romeo Alfetta GTV6 1980-1986
Allard Gold Portfolio 1937-1959
Alvis Gold Portfolio 1919-1967
AMX & Javelin Muscle Portfolio 1968-1974
Armstrong Siddeley Gold Portfolio 1945-1960
Aston Martin Gold Portfolio 1948-1971
Aston Martin Gold Portfolio 1972-1985
Aston Martin Gold Portfolio 1985-1995
Audi Quattro Gold Portfolio 1980-1991
Austin A30 & A35 1951-1962
Austin Healey 100 & 100/6 Gold Port. 1952-1959
Austin Healey 3000 Gold Portfolio 1959-1967
Austin Healey Sprite Gold Portfolio 1958-1971
Barracuda Muscle Portfolio 1964-1974
BMW 1600 Collection No.1 1966-1981
BMW 2002 Gold Portfolio 1968-1976
BMW 316, 318, 320 (4 cyl.) Gold Port. 1975-1990
BMW 320, 323, 325 (6 cyl.) Gold Port. 1977-1990
BMW M Series Performance Portfolio 1976-1993
BMW 5 Series Gold Portfolio 1981-1987
BMW 6 Series Gold Portfolio 1976-1989
Bricklin Gold Portfolio 1974-1975
Bristol Cars Gold Portfolio 1946-1992
Buick Automobiles 1947-1960
Buick Muscle Cars 1965-1970
Cadillac Allanté 1986-1993
Cadillac Automobiles 1949-1959
Cadillac Automobiles 1960-1969
Caprice 1965-1976 ☆ Limited Edition
Charger Muscle Portfolio 1966-1974
Checker ☆ Limited Edition
Chevrolet 1955-1957
Impala & SS Muscle Portfolio 1958-1972
Chevrolet Corvair 1959-1969
Chevy II & Nova SS Muscle Portfolio 1962-1974
Chevy El Camino & SS 1959-1987
Chevelle & SS Muscle Portfolio 1964-1972
Chevrolet Muscle Cars 1966-1971
Chevy Blazer 1969-1981
Chevrolet Corvette Gold Portfolio 1953-1962
Chevrolet Corvette Sting Ray Gold Port. 1963-1967
Chevrolet Corvette Gold Portfolio 1968-1977
High Performance Corvettes 1983-1989
Camaro Muscle Portfolio 1967-1973
Chevrolet Camaro & Z28 1973-1981
High Performance Camaros 1982-1988
Chrysler 300 Gold Portfolio 1955-1970
Chrysler Valiant 1960-1962
Citroen Traction Avant Gold Portfolio 1934-1957
Citroen 2CV Gold Portfolio 1948-1989
Citroen DS & ID 1955-1975
Citroen DS & ID Gold Portfolio 1955-1975
Citroen SM 1970-1975
Cobras & Replicas 1962-1983
Shelby Cobra Gold Portfolio 1962-1969
Cobras & Cobra Replicas Gold Portfolio 1962-1989
Cunningham Automobiles 1951-1955
Daimler SP250 Sports & V-8 250 Saloon Gold P. 1959-1969
Datsun Roadsters 1962-1971
Datsun 240Z 1970-1973
Datsun 280Z & ZX 1975-1983
DeLorean Gold Portfolio 1977-1995
Dodge Muscle Cars 1967-1970
Dodge Viper on the Road
Edsel 1957-1960 ☆ Limited Edition
ERA Gold Portfolio 1934-1994
Excalibur Collection No.1 1952-1981
Facel Vega 1954-1964
Ferrari Dino 1965-1974
Ferrari Dino 308 & Mondial Gold Portfolio1974-1985
Ferrari 328 • 348 • Mondial Gold Portfolio 1986-1994
Fiat 500 Gold Portfolio 1936-1972
Fiat 600 & 850 Gold Portfolio 1955-1972
Fiat Pininfarina 124 & 2000 Spider 1968-1985
Fiat X1/9 Gold Portfolio1973-1989
Fiat Abarth Performance Portfolio 1972-1987
Ford Consul, Zephyr, Zodiac Mk.I & II 1950-1962
Ford Zephyr, Zodiac, Executive, Mk.III & Mk.IV 1962-1971
Ford Cortina 1600E & GT 1967-1970
High Performance Capris Gold Portfolio 1969-1987
Capri Muscle Portfolio 1974-1987
High Performance Fiestas 1979-1991
High Performance Escorts Mk.I 1968-1974
High Performance Escorts Mk.II 1975-1980
High Performance Escorts 1980-1985
High Performance Escorts 1985-1990
High Performance Sierras & Merkurs Gold Portfolio 1983-1990
Ford Automobiles 1949-1959
Ford Fairlane 1955-1970
Ford Ranchero 1957-1959
Ford Thunderbird 1955-1957
Ford Thunderbird 1958-1963
Ford GT40 Gold Portfolio 1964-1987
Ford Bronco 1966-1977
Ford Bronco 1978-1988
Goggomobil ☆ Limited Edition
Holden 1948-1962
Honda CRX 1983-1987
Imperial 1955-1970 ☆ Limited Edition
International Scout Gold Portfolio 1961-1980
Isetta 1953-1964
Iso & Bizzarrini Gold Portfolio 1962-1974
Kaiser • Frazer 1946-1955 ☆ Limited Edition
Jaguar and SS Gold Portfolio 1931-1951
Jaguar XK120, 140, 150 Gold Port. 1948-1960
Jaguar Mk.VII, VIII, IX, X, 420 Gold Port. 1950-1970
Jaguar Mk.1 & Mk.2 Gold Portfolio 1959-1969
Jaguar C-Type & D-Type ☆ Limited Edition
Jaguar E-Type Gold Portfolio 1961-1971
Jaguar E-Type V-12 1971-1975
Jaguar S-Type & 420 ☆ Limited Edition
Jaguar XJ12, XJ5.3, V12 Gold Portfolio 1972-1990
Jaguar XJ6 Series I & II Gold Portfolio 1968-1979
Jaguar XJ6 Series III Perf. Portfolio 1979-1986
Jaguar XJ6 Gold Portfolio 1986-1994
Jaguar XJS Gold Portfolio 1975-1988
Jaguar XJS Gold Portfolio 1988-1995
Jeep CJ5 & CJ6 1960-1976
Jeep CJ5 & CJ7 1976-1986
Jensen Cars 1946-1967
Jensen Cars 1967-1979
Jensen Interceptor Gold Portfolio 1966-1986
Jensen Healey 1972-1976
Lagonda Gold Portfolio 1919-1964
Lamborghini Countach & Urraco 1974-1980
Lamborghini Countach & Jalpa 1980-1985
Lancia Aurelia & Flaminia Gold Portfolio 1950-1970
Lancia Fulvia Gold Portfolio 1963-1976
Lancia Beta Gold Portfolio 1972-1984
Lancia Delta Gold Portfolio 1979-1994
Lancia Stratos 1972-1985
Land Rover Series I 1948-1958
Land Rover Series II & IIa 1958-1971
Land Rover Series III 1971-1985
Land Rover 90 110 Defender Gold Portfolio 1983-1994
Land Rover Discovery 1989-1994
Land Rover Story Part One 1948-1971
Lincoln Gold Portfolio 1949-1960
Lincoln Continental 1961-1969
Lincoln Continental 1969-1976
Lotus Sports Racers Gold Portfolio 1953-1965
Lotus Seven Gold Portfolio 1957-1974
Lotus Caterham Seven Gold Portfolio 1974-1995
Lotus Elan Gold Portfolio 1962-1974
Lotus Elan Collection No. 2 1963-1972
Lotus Elan & SE 1989-1992
Lotus Europa Gold Portfolio 1966-1975
Lotus Elite & Eclat 1974-1982
Lotus Turbo Esprit 1980-1986
Marcos Cars 1960-1988
Maserati 1965-1975
Matra 1965-1983 ☆ Limited Edition
Mazda Miata MX-5 Performance Portfolio 1989-1996
Mazda RX-7 Gold Portfolio 1978-1991
Mercedes 190 & 300 SL 1954-1963
Mercedes G Wagen 1981-1994
Mercedes S & 600 1965-1972
Mercedes S Class 1972-1979
Mercedes 230 • 250 • 280SL Gold Portfolio 1963-1971
Mercedes SLs & SLCs Gold Portfolio 1971-1989
Mercedes SLs Performance Portfolio 1989-1994
Mercury Muscle Cars 1966-1971
Messerschmitt Gold Portfolio 1954-1964
MG Gold Portfolio 1929-1939
MG TA & TC Gold Portfolio 1936-1949
MG TD & TF Gold Portfolio 1949-1955
MGA & Twin Cam Gold Portfolio 1955-1962
MG Midget Gold Portfolio 1961-1979
MGB Roadsters 1962-1980
MGB MGC & V8 Gold Portfolio 1962-1980
MGB GT 1965-1980
MGC & MGB GT V8 ☆ Limited Edition
MG Y-Type & Magnette ZA/ZB ☆ Limited Edition
Mini Gold Portfolio 1959-1969
Mini Gold Portfolio 1969-1980
High Performance Minis Gold Portfolio 1960-1973
Mini Cooper Gold Portfolio 1961-1971
Mini Moke Gold Portfolio 1964-1994
Mopar Muscle Cars 1964-1967
Morgan Three-Wheeler Gold Portfolio 1910-1952
Morgan Plus 4 & Four 4 Gold Portfolio. 1936-1967
Morgan Cars 1960-1970
Morgan Cars Gold Portfolio 1968-1989
Morris Minor Collection No. 1 1948-1980
Shelby Mustang Muscle Portfolio 1965-1970
High Performance Mustang IIs 1974-1978
High Performance Mustangs 1982-1988
Nash & Nash-Healey 1949-1957 ☆ Limited Edition
Nash-Austin Metropolitan Gold Portfolio 1954-1962
Oldsmobile Automobiles 1955-1963
Oldsmobile Muscle Cars 1964-1971
Oldsmobile Toronado 1966-1978
Opel GT Gold Portfolio 1968-1973
Opel Manta 1970-1975 ☆ Limited Edition
Packard Gold Portfolio 1946-1958
Pantera Gold Portfolio 1970-1989
Panther Gold Portfolio 1972-1990
Plymouth Muscle Cars 1966-1971
Pontiac Tempest & GTO 1961-1965
Pontiac Muscle Cars 1966-1972
Pontiac Firebird & Trans-Am 1973-1981
High Performance Firebirds 1982-1988
Pontiac Fiero 1984-1988
Porsche 356 Gold Portfolio 1953-1965
Porsche 911 1965-1969
Porsche 911 1970-1972
Porsche 911 1973-1977
Porsche 911 SC & Turbo Gold Portfolio 1978-1983
Porsche 911 Carrera & Turbo Gold Port. 1984-1989
Porsche 924 Gold Portfolio 1975-1988
Porsche 928 Performance Portfolio 1977-1994
Porsche 944 Gold Portfolio 1981-1991
Range Rover Gold Portfolio 1970-1985
Range Rover Gold Portfolio 1986-1995
Reliant Scimitar 1964-1986
Renault Alpine Gold Portfolio 1958-1994
Riley Gold Portfolio 1924-1939
Rolls Royce Silver Cloud & Bentley 'S' Series Gold Portfolio 1955-1965
Rolls Royce Silver Shadow Gold Port. 1965-1980
Rolls Royce & Bentley Gold Port. 1980-1989
Rover P4 1949-1959
Rover P4 1955-1964
Rover 3 & 3.5 Litre Gold Portfolio 1958-1973
Rover 2000 & 2200 1963-1977
Rover 3500 1968-1977
Rover 3500 & Vitesse 1976-1986
Saab Sonett Collection No.1 1966-1974
Saab Turbo 1976-1983
Studebaker Gold Portfolio 1947-1966
Studebaker Hawks & Larks 1956-1963
Avanti 1962-1990
Sunbeam Tiger & Alpine Gold Portfolio. 1959-1967
Toyota Land Cruiser 1956-1984
Triumph Dolomite Sprint ☆ Limited Edition
Triumph TR2 & TR3 Gold Portfolio 1952-1961
Triumph TR4, TR5, TR250 1961-1968
Triumph TR6 Gold Portfolio 1969-1976
Triumph TR7 & TR8 Gold Portfolio 1975-1982
Triumph Herald 1959-1971
Triumph Vitesse 1962-1971
Triumph Spitfire Gold Portfolio 1962-1980
Triumph 2000, 2.5, 2500 1963-1977
Triumph GT6 Gold Portfolio 1966-1974
Triumph Stag Gold Portfolio 1970-1977
TVR Gold Portfolio 1959-1986
TVR Performance Portfolio 1986-1994
VW Beetle Gold Portfolio 1935-1967
VW Beetle Gold Portfolio 1968-1991
VW Beetle Collection No.1 1970-1982
VW Karmann Ghia 1955-1982
VW Bus, Camper, Van 1954-1967
VW Bus, Camper, Van 1968-1979
VW Bus, Camper, Van 1979-1989
VW Scirocco 1974-1981
VW Golf GTI 1976-1986
Volvo PV444 & PV544 1945-1965
Volvo Amazon-120 Gold Portfolio 1956-1970
Volvo 1800 Gold Portfolio 1960-1973
Volvo 140 & 160 Series Gold Portfolio 1966-1975
Westfield ☆ Limited Edition

Forty Years of Selling Volvo

BROOKLANDS ROAD & TRACK SERIES

Road & Track on Alfa Romeo 1964-1970
Road & Track on Alfa Romeo 1971-1976
Road & Track on Aston Martin 1962-1990
R & T on Auburn Cord and Duesenburg 1952-84
Road & Track on Audi & Auto Union 1952-1980
Road & Track on Audi & Auto Union 1980-1986
Road & Track on Austin Healey 1953-1970
Road & Track on BMW Cars 1966-1974
Road & Track on BMW Cars 1975-1978
Road & Track on BMW Cars 1979-1983
R & T on Cobra, Shelby & Ford GT40 1962-1992
Road & Track on Corvette 1953-1967
Road & Track on Corvette 1968-1982
Road & Track on Corvette 1982-1986
Road & Track on Corvette 1986-1990
Road & Track on Ferrari 1975-1981
Road & Track on Ferrari 1981-1984
Road & Track on Ferrari 1984-1988
Road & Track on Fiat Sports Cars 1968-1987
Road & Track on Jaguar 1950-1960
Road & Track on Jaguar 1961-1968
Road & Track on Jaguar 1968-1974
Road & Track on Jaguar 1974-1982
Road & Track on Jaguar 1983-1989
Road & Track on Lamborghini 1964-1985
Road & Track on Lotus 1972-1981
Road & Track on Maserati 1975-1983
R & T on Mazda RX-7 & MX-5 Miata 1986-1991
Road & Track on Mercedes 1952-1962
Road & Track on Mercedes 1963-1970
Road & Track on Mercedes 1971-1979
Road & Track on Mercedes 1980-1987
Road & Track on MG Sports Cars 1949-1961
Road & Track on MG Sports Cars 1962-1980
Road & Track on Mustang 1964-1977
R & T on Nissan 300-ZX & Turbo 1984-1989
Road & Track on Pontiac 1960-1983
Road & Track on Porsche 1951-1967
Road & Track on Porsche 1968-1971
Road & Track on Porsche 1972-1975
Road & Track on Porsche 1975-1978
Road & Track on Porsche 1979-1982
Road & Track on Porsche 1985-1988
R & T on Rolls Royce & Bentley 1950-1965
R & T on Rolls Royce & Bentley 1966-1984
Road & Track on Saab 1972-1992
R & T on Toyota Sports & GT Cars 1966-1984
R & T on Triumph Sports Cars 1953-1967
R & T on Triumph Sports Cars 1967-1974
R & T on Triumph Sports Cars 1974-1982
Road & Track on Volkswagen 1951-1968
Road & Track on Volkswagen 1968-1978
Road & Track on Volkswagen 1978-1985
Road & Track on Volvo 1957-1974
Road & Track on Volvo 1977-1994
R & T - Henry Manney at Large & Abroad
R & T - Peter Egan's "Side Glances"
R & T - Peter Egan "At Large"

BROOKLANDS CAR AND DRIVER SERIES

Car and Driver on BMW 1955-1977
Car and Driver on BMW 1977-1985
C and D on Cobra, Shelby & Ford GT40 1963-84
Car and Driver on Corvette 1978-1982
Car and Driver on Corvette 1983-1988
C and D on Datsun Z 1600 & 2000 1966-1984
Car and Driver on Ferrari 1955-1962
Car and Driver on Ferrari 1963-1975
Car and Driver on Ferrari 1976-1983
Car and Driver on Mopar 1956-1967
Car and Driver on Mopar 1968-1975
Car and Driver on Mustang 1964-1972
Car and Driver on Pontiac 1961-1975
Car and Driver on Porsche 1955-1962
Car and Driver on Porsche 1963-1970
Car and Driver on Porsche 1970-1976
Car and Driver on Porsche 1977-1981
Car and Driver on Porsche 1982-1986
Car and Driver on Saab 1956-1985
Car and Driver on Volvo 1955-1986

BROOKLANDS PRACTICAL CLASSICS SERIES

PC on Austin A40 Restoration
PC on Land Rover Restoration
PC on Metalworking in Restoration
PC on Midget/Sprite Restoration
PC on MGB Restoration
PC on Sunbeam Rapier Restoration
PC on Triumph Herald/Vitesse
PC on Spitfire Restoration
PC on Beetle Restoration
PC on 1930s Car Restoration

BROOKLANDS HOT ROD 'MUSCLECAR & HI-PO ENGINES' SERIES

Chevy 265 & 283
Chevy 302 & 327
Chevy 348 & 409
Chevy 350 & 400
Chevy 396 & 427
Chevy 454 thru 512
Chrysler Hemi
Chrysler 273, 318, 340 & 360
Chrysler 361, 383, 400, 413, 426, 440
Ford 289, 302, Boss 302 & 351W
Ford 351C & Boss 351
Ford Big Block

BROOKLANDS RESTORATION SERIES

Auto Restoration Tips & Techniques
Basic Bodywork Tips & Techniques
Camaro Restoration Tips & Techniques
Chevrolet High Performance Tips & Techniques
Chevy Engine Swapping Tips & Techniques
Chevy-GMC Pickup Repair
Chrysler Engine Swapping Tips & Techniques
Engine Swapping Tips & Techniques
Ford Pickup Repair
How to Build a Street Rod
Land Rover Restoration Tips & Techniques
MG 'T' Series Restoration Guide
MGA Restoration Guide
Mustang Restoration Tips & Techniques
Performance Tuning - Chevrolets of the '60s
Performance Tuning - Pontiacs of the '60s

MOTORCYCLING

BROOKLANDS ROAD TEST SERIES

AJS & Matchless Gold Portfolio 1945-1966
BSA Twins A7 & A10 Gold Portfolio 1946-1962
BSA Twins A50 & A65 Gold Portfolio 1962-1973
Ducati Gold Portfolio 1960-1974
Ducati Gold Portfolio 1974-1978
Laverda Gold Portfolio 1967-1977
Norton Commando Gold Portfolio 1968-1977
Triumph Bonneville Gold Portfolio 1959-1983

BROOKLANDS CYCLE WORLD SERIES

Cycle World on BMW 1974-1980
Cycle World on BMW 1981-1986
Cycle World on Ducati 1982-1991
Cycle World on Harley-Davidson 1962-1968
Cycle World on Harley-Davidson 1978-1983
Cycle World on Harley-Davidson 1983-1987
Cycle World on Harley-Davidson 1987-1990
Cycle World on Harley-Davidson 1990-1992
Cycle World on Honda 1962-1967
Cycle World on Honda 1968-1971
Cycle World on Honda 1971-1974
Cycle World on Husqvarna 1966-1976
Cycle World on Husqvarna 1977-1984
Cycle World on Kawasaki 1966-1971
Cycle World on Kawasaki Off-Road Bikes 1972-1979
Cycle World on Kawasaki Street Bikes 1972-1976
Cycle World on Norton 1962-1971
Cycle World on Suzuki 1962-1970
Cycle World on Suzuki Off-Road Bikes 1971-1976
Cycle World on Suzuki Street Bikes 1971-1976
Cycle World on Triumph 1967-1972
Cycle World on Yamaha 1962-1969
Cycle World on Yamaha Off-Road Bikes 1970-1974
Cycle World on Yamaha Street Bikes 1970-1974

MILITARY

BROOKLANDS MILITARY VEHICLES SERIES

Allied Military Vehicles No.2 1941-1946
Complete WW2 Military Jeep Manual
Dodge Military Vehicles No.1 1940-1945
Hail To The Jeep
Military & Civilian Amphibians 1940-1990
Off Road Jeeps: Civ. & Mil. 1944-1971
US Military Vehicles 1941-1945
US Army Military Vehicles WW2-TM9-2800
VW Kubelwagen Military Portfolio 1940-1990
WW 2 Jeep Military Portfolio 1941-1945

RACING

Le Mans - The Jaguar Years - 1949-1957
Le Mans - The Ferrari Years - 1958-1965
Le Mans - The Ford & Matra Years - 1966-1974

19126

CONTENTS

ACKNOWLEDGEMENTS

For more than 35 years, Brooklands Books have been publishing compilations of road tests and other articles from the English speaking world's leading motoring magazines. We have already published more than 600 titles, and in these we have made available to motoring enthusiasts some 20,000 stories which would otherwise have become hard to find. For the most part, our books focus on a single model, and as such they have become an invaluable source of information. As Bill Boddy of *Motor Sport* was kind enough to write when reviewing one of our Gold Portfolio volumes, the Brooklands catalogue "must now constitute the most complete historical source of reference available, at least of the more recent makes and models."

Even so, we are constantly being asked to publish new titles on cars which have a narrower appeal than those we have already covered in our main series. The economics of book production make it impossible to cover these subjects in our main series, but Limited Edition volumes like this one give us a way to tackle these less popular but no less worthy subjects. This additional range of books is matched by a Limited Edition - Extra series, which contains volumes with further material to supplement existing titles in our Road Test and Gold Portfolio ranges.

Both the Limited Edition and Limited Edition - Extra series maintain the same high standards of presentation and reproduction set by our established ranges. However, each volume is printed in smaller quantities - which is perhaps the best reason we can think of why you should buy this book now. We would also like to remind readers that we are always open to suggestions for new titles; perhaps your club or interest group would like us to consider a book on your particular subject?

Our thanks go to Chris Smith of Westfield Sportscars Limited, for supplying the photographs that grace our front and back covers and also for his invaluable advice in the preparation of this book.

Finally, we are more than pleased to acknowledge that Brooklands Books rely on the help and co-operation of those who publish the magazines where the articles in our books originally appeared. For this present volume, we gratefully acknowledge the continued support of the publishers of *Autocar, Autosport, Auto Performance, Cars & Car Conversions, Classic and Sportscar, Complete Car, Fast Lane, Modern Motor, Motor Sport, Perfomance Car, Perfomance Tuning, Road & Track, Sports Car Illustrated, Supercar Classics, Top Gear* and *Westfield* for allowing us to include their valuable and informative copyright stories.

R.M. Clarke.

Westfield sunrise

MARCUS PYE recently enjoyed a nostalgic day in Chris Smith's modern classics.

Kit cars as such are not a new concept. They have been around now for some 25 years, but the escalating cost of new mass-produced vehicles, the relative lack of genuine fun cars and man's insatiable quest to stand out from the crowd in this era of stereotyped hatchbacks and company 'three box' transport, has seen this sector of the market flourish beyond recognition, particularly over the past decade.

The 1950s and '60s brought an interesting variety of do-it-yourself sports machinery from the Falcon and Rochdale to the stylish Marcos. The American dune buggy craze swept Britain next, fading almost as quickly as it had erupted, leaving a trail of derelict small businesses in its wake. Sports cars were back in vogue for the '70s with the Imp-powered Davrian, Ginetta and Clan leading the way, before Tim Dutton-Woolley finally found what the punters wanted. His ultra-cheap and, not surprisingly, rudimentary Dutton roadsters have brought him fame, fortune (and a Lamborghini Countach!) and continue to sell faster than he can produce them.

Following the mock-exotica period in which the elegant Nova (based, like so many other kits, on the ubiquitous VW Beetle running gear) led the way, manufacturers looked increasingly toward timeless classic designs for their inspiration. Soon a plethora of 'replicars' — so called because most bear a close resemblance to the original rather than being faithful replicas — was available. Now anyone could own an AC Cobra, a D-type Jaguar, a Ferrari Testa Rossa or 250LM, a Porsche Spyder, a Ford GT40 or even a Bugatti T35 in the eyes of his uninitiated neighbour.

Chris Smith is, unashamedly, an out-and-out Lotus freak. Countless successes on the racing circuits of Europe, the majority in Lotus 6, 10 and 17 models of Colin Chapman's design, bear testament to this and his business at Armitage in the heart of the Black Country has long specialised in the restoration, preparation and sale of these marvellous examples of the *marque*.

In the spring of this year Smith asked himself whether there was room in the depressed motor market for a contemporary sports car of a similar nature of those he knew so well. One further look at the constant stream of anonymous saloons on the roads of his native West Midlands was sufficient to fire his enthusiasm.

Top: Like the sleek Lotus Eleven which it resembles, the intriguing Westfield Sports car is available in two distinctive body styles. The striking red production car sports the optional aerodynamic head-fairing and aluminium chassis panniers in contrast to the straight touring tail section of the glass-fibre podded BRG demonstrator. Left: Access to the 'Spridget'-oriented running gear is excellent, allowing easy maintenance. All panels are completely detachable.

Onlookers were receptive to Chris's initiative from the moment his prototype first turned a wheel and it appealed instantly to a couple of friends, who longed to rediscover the joys of open-air motoring. Suitably encouraged, Smith founded Westfield Sports Cars with the intention of producing and marketing complete vehicles to customers' specifications.

To be really successful in this highly individual field, a manufacturer must take into account a number of basic criteria. The visual appeal of the finished article is obviously important, especially when impulse plays such a large part in selection of cars to many people, but the practicalities of chassis durability, component availability, ease of assembly and maintenance, must be carefully considered and exhaustively thought out, in relation to quality and value-for-money — probably the greatest sale-clincher in these cost-conscious days.

Smith and his small staff at Westfield are in business not only to fill what they consider to be an inviting void in the sports and fun car market, but also to survive by offering an unusual and well engineered commodity at a price which comes within reach of many. Originally, it was intended to build every car on the premises with new components for an inclusive price of £4542 (3950 + VAT). The level of interest was overwhelming, but as soon as statistics proved that a large proportion of enquiries were coming from teenagers and the younger enthusiast, Chris revised his marketing strategy, introducing kit options from £1777.50 inc VAT and opening his doors still wider.

Any MG Midget or Austin-Healey Sprite derivative, (Smith has also raced a Sprite with distinction by the way), is ripe for conversion into a Westfield, providing that it is mechanically sound. The condition of the body/chassis unit is unimportant as it is entirely surplus to requirements. Rusty, tatty, or damaged Spridgets are in plentiful supply, even at under £300, and one might prefer to seek out a pre-'63 base car if the new 'classic' is to retain an 'authentic' non-suffix registration plate.

Engine, gearbox, drive train and most of the running gear and ancillaries must be transferred to the Westfield's strong tubular steel spaceframe chassis, jig welded to Smith's design by an ex-Arch Motors craftsman. Those of you unfamiliar with FF1600 racing, may be unaware of Arch's enviable reputation in their field, so precision and quality of finish can be assured.

The chassis itself is stove enamelled on delivery and is supplied to kit customers with a complete set of pre-cut aluminium sheeting ready for panelling. For a small additional charge, Westfield will bond and rivet the panels and fit the neat rolled aluminium rear bulkhead to give a central 'tub' of monocoque-like strength and rigidity. An arduous and exacting task best left to the experts methinks, particularly if you are susceptible to bouts of rivetgunner's thumb!

Once the chassis is finished and sitting on trestles in the garage (or on prospective mother-in-law's patio should the fancy take you), the assembly can begin in earnest. The engine is mounted on three rubber bushes and the gearbox slots neatly into the transmission tunnel, although exchange propshaft and rear live axle will have to be obtained from the factory following custom modification to suit the Westfield installation by Hardy Spicer.

Front suspension is by lower wishbone and single top link with anti-roll bar — all included in the kit of parts — while the rear axle is located by twin trailing arms and a Panhard rod. Specially rated Spax spring/damper units are recommended. Steering box, pedal assembly, wiring loom and dash panel are all taken directly from the donor vehicle and the radiator refitted in the nose cowling. The battery sits in the front left pannier tray, behind the wheelarch, while the exhaust system runs down the opposite flank.

Although the standard Spridget fuel tank may be retained, a more compact welded aluminium one with 'Monza' filler is available to slit into the tail of the car. Not included in the cost of the basic kit are such necessities as lights (which can come from the old car), windscreen and interior trim, which the budget-builder can buy as his car nears completion. MGB knock-on wire wheels of 4½in width are desirable for a truly original appearance.

The timeless lines of the Westfield add to its great charm and popularity with the fresh air addict.

The tough self-coloured glass fibre bodywork is moulded in five sections — bonnet, cockpit, doors and tail — although the lower panniers can be specified in this material or aluminium according to preference. The body closely follows the Lotus Eleven's aesthetically and aerodynamically pleasing lines, (indeed the Westfield's wheelbase and track dimensions are virtually the same as the original masterpiece), and may be ordered in standard touring trim or with the striking head-fairing which, back in the '50s, was added to aid high speed stability on some racing Elevens.

Chris has not produced the Westfield as a Lotus Eleven replica, more a practical and enjoyable modern sports car with its character projected through sporting legend, but, not unnaturally, many owners will regard their Westfields in the hallowed tones of yesteryear and why not, for it is a very fine venture in many respects. Bearing in mind that the car has been developed over a period of only three months, Smith's achievement is all the more remarkable in that the Westfield appears to have no bugs, merely one or two very minor shortcomings, which, in the eyes of its owners, may well enhance the car's charisma.

Many owners will opt for the 'racing' tail fin.

I had the opportunity to drive both the green 'works prototype' sports version and the red finned customer car in the Donington area last month and, typically, the British climate was at its most inclement, as it often tends to be when magazines arrange to test open machinery. The intrepid Smith and his assistant duly arrived having puddle-jumped their way from base, an hour distant. Wringing wet, yet beaming with pleasure — weather equipment is under development for the Westfield to alleviate the problem — they sponged out the cockpits prior to handing the cars over the AUTOSPORT. Mercifully, the rain stopped later and the potential of the Westield was easier to ascertain.

A small crowd of people were gazing incredulously at the sleek, low-slung car when we commenced business — the Westfield owner will quickly find himself the centre of attention, whether the car is seen at the pub, in the high street, or on the open road. The sight of a diminutive racing car roaring past, causes something approaching apoplexy in the average Marina enthusiast (!) imprisoned in a clammy passenger cell, while Westfield occupants enjoy Chris Smith's own brand of wind-in-the-face, exhilaration at half the price.

The small doors hinge downwards for ease of entry to the spartan, but surprisingly spacious, interior of the '50s racer but the more virile owner will doubtless prefer to clamber over the sidescreen before sliding down beneath the red leather-rimmed 14in wheel, synonymous with sports cars of the original era. Wide sills and a sturdy transmission tunnel endow the Westfield with rather more torsional stiffness than the car which it resembles on the surface. They also contrive to hold passengers firmly in their seats under cornering without restricting movement in any way. Thin, but surprisingly comfortable upholstery, cushions occupants most satisfactorily — and drivers of 6ft 6ins can be accommodated behind the wheel with minimal adjustment to the pedal box.

All-round visibility is unimpaired with the 'flat' bodywork, making the Westfield a doddle to place on the road or manoeuvre in tight spaces, while the racing fin detracts little from this happy state of affairs. Steering lock on the production car was impressive considering that the front wheels are faired in, making it very easy to drive for experienced and novice pilots alike.

As soon as the engine is started, one knows that the Westfield is properly engineered, for, unlike some 'kit cars', the chassis remains virtually free of vibration. Pedal operation is comfortably weighted and the car glides effortlessly away, whether trickling or under full power. The gearchange is light and precise on the

Although spartan the cockpit is roomy, practical and not uncomfortable. Trim pack is at extra cost.

production car, although a more deliberate stab was required in the well-used demonstrator.

Performance of the older car was certainly adequate with its 120,000-mile engine being given a new lease of life in the Westfield chassis. Weighing-in at a shade over 500kgs, (around 9cwt unladen), the car is a good deal lighter than its MG Midget ancestor, with corresponding improvement in both performance and retardation. The standard Midget brakes, discs in front, drums behind, stop the car very quickly indeed.

Acceleration is, of course, better too, particularly if the engine is revved to its 7000rpm red-line in the intermediate gears, the green car emitting a glorious burble due to its straight-through exhaust.

Although less noisy with its BSA motorcycle silencer, the red Westfield was significantly quicker with its newer mechanicals, without resorting to optional lower differential gearing than the 4.2 final drive of the demonstrator. A range of diffs is available ex-factory, depending on whether it's performance or economy you require. As an indication, recent fuel consumption tests on the prototype have proved a miserly 60mpg to be attainable while the red version has recorded 0-60mph times of around 9secs. Both cars top 100mph with ease, a maximum of over 120mph being possible with suitable gearing.

The handling of the Westfield is well up to its performance, chassis sorting being another of Smith's personal fortés. Taut suspension gives a firm, though not harsh, ride and the car's comparatively wide track allows surefooted cornering and roadholding despite the relatively skinny tyres. The Westfield can be safely thrown into a corner to counter a slight in-built tendency to understeer (inherently safer than oversteer) and will come out with its tail hanging mildly out of line, balanced on the throttle. When oversteer is induced, it is in no way violent and simply self-corrects as the little car surges towards the next corner.

Tractable and fun come rain or shine the car could be bettered only in minor detail. Of course many potential owners will want a hood or at least a tonneau cover to repel the worst of the British climate and both are being worked upon as priorities by Westfield Sports Cars. A solid tonneau and perhaps even a monoposto cockpit surround to match the head fairing may be offered too, although the hood assembly would require the fitment of a full-sized windscreen which may look ungainly on the car. Many owners, I feel, will be running Westfields as second cars anyway, so the question of regular wet weather use may not arise.

Smith is currently striving to improve the fit of the body panels, particularly the bonnet, which is wide and unsupported where it meets the scuttle. The glass fibre work is a quality moulding and all parts are easily detached from the chassis to facilitate unimpeded maintenance. The bonnet and 'boot', (there is no luggage space as such, but a small holdall could probably be attached to the fuel tank with bungy straps for occasional runs), hinge outwards in everyday use with jack sockets to disconnect the lights for removal. An extended petrol filler neck is being worked on to enable refuelling to take place without opening the back. Lighting is said to be satisfactory, although we did not try the cars after dark, headlamps being faired-in by perspex covers.

So much thought has gone into perfecting the Westfield that it is hard to think of ways to improve it further. Certainly it is a great deal better than a Spridget in the handling and braking departments, it is no more uncomfortable and has a sensible driving position if practicality is sacrificed. Day to day running will be easier and, importantly, it will not rust. Spares and repairs will be readily available and inexpensive (a new BL Gold Seal engine is under £200) and insurance, through a specialist sports/kit car broker such as Adrian Flux, only fractionally more than the old base car. For individuality and exclusivity — only 250 odd genuine Lotus Elevens were built remember — a Westfield could be put on the road for little over £2000 plus a couple of weeks' toil in the garage. It seems a small price to pay for such a status symbol, especially since the quality of engineering should guarantee its enjoyment will last for many years.

Response from the American market has been incredible, each post bringing fresh orders from California in particular, where Westfields will shortly be buzzing round daily without fear of rain. At home too, a fair number of rotting Spridgets will become sparkling new Westfields over the winter if the weight of the Armitage postman's sack each morning is anything to go by.

Smith has clearly got the recipe right with quality, styling and mechanical simplicity at a price people can, and will, afford. A new tail moulding incorporating the fin has been plugged — a riveted aluminium fairing is fitted to the red car at present — and I feel this version will capture the hearts of potential buyers, as it did mine. Its macho racing image and ageless, balanced lines, are beautiful in comparison to the functional and stubbier-looking flat deck sportster.

I am tempted indeed to order a car, in British Racing Green with aluminium underbelly. Add white number roundels and a yellow pinstripe with 'Team Lotus' picked out each side of the cockpit and all but the local historian need never know that the car is not the 1957 Le Mans class-winning chassis. Or one can sit at home dreaming of competing in Les Vingt Quatre Heures du Haywards Heath . . . or St Albans . . . or Walsall but better still, visit Westfield Sports Cars — and order your leather flying helmet and goggles on the way home. You'll be needing them! ∎

Above, left to right: Rear axle location, engine installation and tourer. Below: the handsome finned car.

WESTFIELD SPORTS
£1550 plus VAT, kit form; £3950 plus VAT complete

Specification
Chassis	tubular steel spaceframe
Final drive	optional radios available from 3.7-5.3:1
Steering	rack and pinion
Brakes	discs front/drums rear
Wheels	4½J knock-on 14in wire rims; ex-factory
Tyres	to customer choice
Suspension (F)	independent wishbone, top link, coilspring/damper, anti-roll bar.
(R)	live axle, parallel trailing arms, coilspring/damper and Panhard rod.

(Mechanical specification and performance dependant on Austin-Healey Sprite/MG Midget base car for engine, gearbox and rear axle ratio.)

Dimensions
Wheelbase	88ins
Track (F/R)	45.5ins/45ins
Length	138.7ins
Width	60ins
Weight	approx 9cwt

WESTFIELD SPORTS CAR

A Lotus 11 look-alike springs into action

BY DOUG NYE
PHOTOS BY GEOFFREY GODDARD

Remember when sports car interiors offered a minimum of fuss and a maximum of fun?'

Front suspension is an adjustable independent design. Recommended drivetrain is a 1275-cc Spridget 4-cylinder and 4-speed gearbox.

AMPLING WHAT MIGHT be described as enthusiasts' kit cars can be a dubious pleasure. You have a duty to your readers to tell the truth and it sometimes comes hard to break the bad news to the optimistic constructor. He might be a pleasant enough chap, but if you've just frightened yourself half to death, been soaked, frozen, perhaps sprayed with hot oil or water and sustained extensive bruising plus lost tooth fillings, you might not be at all charitable about the project to which he has devoted himself and his life savings.

So, you wait, one day, some day, for a good kit car to pop up. Occasionally it happens, and it's always a pleasure to report the good news. When I was first asked to try the Lotus 11-based Westfield sports car, the question was simply, "Is it any good?" Now, despite another of those cold, mist-shrouded, rain-dampened English winter days, it's nice to say, unequivocally, "Yes, it is good, very good indeed." In fact, it's rather special.

The car is produced by Chris Smith's Westfield Sports Cars company in a tiny industrial unit at Dudley in the heart of England's industrial Midlands. Chris has for many years been a very active dealer in racing cars. He raced MGs, a Lotus 6 and more recently a Lotus 17 sports car in historic events and built quite a reputation as a capable preparer of such machines. In March 1982 he was driving an old American business associate, Mark Hancock, from Roanoke, Virginia, up to Manchester in a Cooper S that Mark had just purchased from him. They were on the way to view an MG TC and were discussing a rusting original Lotus 11 frame lying in the garden of Chris's home, Westfield House. Hancock wondered if it would be possible to build up the frame into a usable road car. Chris felt it was beyond salvation and the best course would be to make a new frame from scratch. If he was to do that at all, it might be worth modifying the original design to make it more practical for modern tastes and road conditions; in short, to build a near look-alike replica. The idea for the Westfield sports car was born.

The project progressed incredibly quickly. By June a prototype had been completed and was being sorted out by its creator. There was an immediate flood of interest in the UK and abroad. In August, Willard Howe of Rev-Pro Engineering, Inc in Sarasota, Florida, confirmed his enthusiasm with a cash order and soon became U.S. agent for the cars, now named after Chris Smith's house. "If you've ever struggled to find a name for a car, you'll understand why! There's a Westfield Bend at Brands Hatch and it seemed to have the right connotations and the right period sound. The setting-sun badge we designed for the car was obviously the next step—the sun sets in the west after all."

Now just a year after the project's inception, the tiny Dudley works with its staff of seven is inundated with orders and has proved well capable of meeting them. Chris' original guess that he might sell two dozen cars over a period of years has already been far-outdistanced. While six or so have gone to British customers more than three times that number have been sold for export and many more are following.

The Westfield is not in truth a replica of Colin Chapman's supremely successful 1956–1957 sports-racing car. It really *is* an all-new sports car carrying look-alike fiberglass bodywork. We've heard that all before and it probably sounds rather tacky. What makes the Westfield different is its sound engineering: It goes as well as it looks and it has civilized good manners and a well developed comfortable character that, on the open road, the original highly strung Lotus could never match.

The key to the Westfield's comfortingly solid feel is the redesigned multi-tubular spaceframe chassis. While the lightweight Lotus original was sufficient for racing success, its 20-gauge round-tube construction was somewhat marginal for everyday or even fun-car motoring on the open road unless the owner had regular access to a welding set. The Westfield frame is much more robust, being welded-up in 16-gauge tube, the vast majority 1-in. and ¾-in. square section mild steel with just five small low stressed numbers in ¾-in. round stock. The use of square-section tube aids attachment of body-paneling and stressed-skin sections, and the fully framed transmission tunnel adds considerable extra strength in beam and torsion. This bare frame is paneled in 16- and 18-gauge aluminum sheet. The undertray encloses all mechanical parts from the edge of the rear body-work to the engine compartment.

Front suspension is fully independent (mirroring the Lotus 11 Series II rather than the split-axle Series 1 layout) with double tubular wishbones and Spax coil-spring shock absorbers with ride-height and stiffness adjustment. The front camber angle, set standard at ½ degree positive, is also adjustable.

At the rear Chris chose a live axle (like the Lotus 11 Club basic model) located by twin parallel radius rods on either side and a lateral Panhard rod. Spax coil shock absorber units are featured again.

Lockheed 8.2-in. front disc brakes are used, matched with 7.0-in. diameter rear drums. Steering is by rack and pinion with a double universal-joint steering column and a Westfield-reproduced 14-in. Lotus-type steering wheel trimmed as original in red leather over a 3-spoke aluminum spider.

The standard power unit is the 1275-cc BL 4-cylinder engine from the Sprite/Midget sports car series. It's matched to a 4-speed gearbox as in the Spridgets. This engine, using twin 1¾-in. SU carburetors, develops around 65 bhp. One original idea behind the project was to supply the chassis/body kit to the owner of a rotted-out Spridget, who could then recondition his existing engine, gearbox, back axle and brakes and transfer them to the new frame. It soon became apparent that the market was far wider than owners of rotted-out Spridgets, and complete kits or fully assembled Westfield cars are now being produced with as-new mechanical parts from the BL spares shelves plus a wide range of alternative power units and other mechanical parts.

The Dudley works has tailored its new square-tube spaceframe chassis to accommodate twincam Lotus-Ford, Mazda RX-7, Vauxhall Chevette and Fiat twincam engines. Such custom-built freedom is fine while numbers are small, but Chris Smith is wary of going too far down such a custom-build road: "We could find ourselves spending all our time developing specials instead of producing what we know works well."

Just how well I discovered in the mist and drizzle of the Black Country when I drove a red customer car with its appropriately pre-1963 registration 737 FUE. Its owner lives "just around the

WESTFIELD

corner" and his car is regularly used as a demonstrator alongside the green original works prototype VTL 715 with its rather hotter engine and open exhaust.

The fiberglass body panels hinge open clamshell-style front and rear, exposing fuel tank and engine bay to give excellent access. To improve it further they easily detach completely. The tiny doors each swing down as on the Lotus but normally you just don't bother, merely step over them into the wider-than-11 cockpit, stand on the floor cross-tube just ahead of the nicely trimmed seat cushion, straighten your legs and slither down beneath the red-rimmed wheel.

Now being broad in the beam, I tend to jam about 2-in. above the seat in a Lotus 11. In the Westfield I quite comfortably struck bottom. Leg room is a little restricted for a 6-footer, though Chris is 6 ft 2 in. and he fit into the slightly more roomy prototype car quite comfortably. It has a different pedal layout, which is now standard in production and although big feet can muddle throttle and brake together, one quickly becomes acclimated.

The privately owned Westfield started and ran with a civilized drone from its BSA motorcycle silencer, sounding absolutely Spridget and unobtrusive. The gear change with its stubby central lever is quick, short and neat: clean gate and no confusion. The steering is Porsche-like in its directness and feel, not as nervous as the last genuine Lotus 11 I drove, and much improved because of that. The car rides on 4½-in. MGB wire

wheels and 145-14 steel-braced radial tires and this is one key to its impeccable road manners. Wider wheels and tires, in fact, would spoil the car. It's still very light in relative terms, weighing around 1100 lb, and those narrow footprint tires allow it to run arrow-straight, hands-off on poorish road surfaces without any tendency to "white-line" and wander.

Tests proved that use of very low, 18-psi, tire pressure with quite firm settings on the adjustable shock absorbers gave a very comfortable ride and this by itself is one of the car's most endearing features. This isn't the usual rock-hard bone-shaker, and because it's so light it still does not attempt to roll off its low-pressure tires—and in corners it's as much fun as an open-wheel Caterham Seven or a Lotus 7 original: You just set it up, take aim and wrist-steer the car through on the throttle. And being light, and such a slippery shape, it is very quick. On the wet and greasy road surfaces around Dudley it was easy to break traction with power on those narrow rear wheels but there was always ample warning to catch oversteering slides—intentionally provoked or otherwise—and indeed sustain them with that admirable steering and responsive throttle. In fact, the car is essentially a mild understeerer in the best Chapman fashion and it always felt stable and friendly, not a car that was about to turn around and bite you because of a moment's inattention. Of course, one penalty of light weight and quite powerful brakes in such conditions is lockup, but the application had to be hard and on pumping the pedal they unlocked and the tires gripped adequately to prevent a too-instructive view of the underside of the truck ahead. You do sit very low.

Essentially this is a fun car for fair-weather motoring, just like the illustrious Lotus it emulates. I was surprised how little rain entered the cockpit although it was running up the low plastic

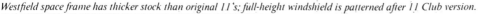

Westfield space frame has thicker stock than original 11's; full-height windshield is patterned after 11 Club version.

WESTFIELD

windscreen in rivers and spraying back onto my face. When you're my size it's hard to hunch down out of the airstream, and then without wipers you cannot see through the screen. But the original Lotus 11 Club offered as optional a tall fixed glass screen, with a usable top to match, and similar equipment is being rushed through now for the Westfield range.

Despite the dampness, I loved every minute of my drives in both cars. There was no opportunity for performance timing but they cruise quietly and very comfortably—that is the surprise—at legal limits and will exceed 100 mph unflustered and without the body flapping and clattering as of old. The whole impression is of a solid well developed little car that won't spoil your day. And on a long run the standard engine returns more than 50 mpg; it's pulling minimal weight and has an aerodynamically efficient body shape.

The only criticisms I have of the cars I drove is of their early fiberglass body panels that fit rather poorly and whose finish is less than excellent, while being adequate on a specialist fun car.

But now consider the price, because here in the UK the Westfield springs its greatest surprise when the majority of enthusiasts find they can afford it! The basic complete kit sells for only £1550 ($2600), while fully assembled the price is only £4250 ($7000). These price levels are simply a steal, you cannot buy a decent small sedan for that, yet here we have a genuine, usable, comfortable 100-mph sports car tailored for around town driving or long-distance motoring, whichever takes your fancy.

The basic kit includes everything in bare form. Electrophoretic powder-coat chassis painting can be included in the kit price for an extra £75, and the Dudley works will fit all chassis paneling for only another £100. If the customer wants the trim pack professionally fitted that's only another £95, and for £120 the optional aluminum sill panels—Chris insists they are called pontoons—replace the basic fiberglass sections. For around £2000 an Englishman can buy a 100-mph 2-seat sports car that could be easily completed in his home garage within days. And, for once I have no doubts that claim is true.

There is good news for you enthusiasts in America too. Willard Howe has received his initial order and says the kits start at around $4000 and depending on the equipment and engine specification go up to approximately $10,500 for the completed car constructed by Rev-Pro Engineering. For more information, contact Willard Howe, Rev-Pro Engineering, Inc, 6223 S. McIntosh Rd, Sarasota, Fla. 33583; 813 922-7371.

Amongst Westfield's options beyond the basics are deluxe trim with carpeting and side-panel cockpit trim, and an as-original Lotus 11 head-fairing, which is a far more attractive shape than the rather hideous early fairing on the red car I drove. There is also a close-ratio gearbox offered, plus a modified Spridget engine, which for around £600 is taken out to more than 1340 cc, fitted with a big-valve head and balancing internals and is good for more than 7000 rpm and 100 bhp.

Frankly I would have reservations about squeezing too much power into the Westfield as it stands, not through any doubts about its structural capacity to cope but because I feel it would probably upset its excellent balance. The Westfield sports is simply the best-developed and most attractive new sports car I have had the pleasure to drive for many a long year.

WESTFIELD EUROPEAN SPECIFICATIONS

GENERAL

Curb weight, lb/kg	1100	500
Wheelbase, in./mm	88.0	2235
Track, front/rear	45.5/45.0	1156/1143
Length	138.8	3525
Width	60.0	1524
Height	34.0	864
Fuel capacity, U.S. gal./liters	5.0	18.9

ENGINE

Type	ohv inline-4
Bore x stroke, in./mm	2.78 x 3.20....70.5 x 81.2
Displacement, cu in./cc	77.8.......1275
Compression ratio	9.0:1
Bhp @ rpm, SAE net/kW	65/48 @ 5500
Torque @ rpm, lb-ft/Nm	78/106 @ 3000
Carburetion	two SU (1V)

DRIVETRAIN

Transmission	4-sp manual
Gear ratios: 4th (1.00)	4.22:1
3rd (1.43)	6.03:1
2nd (2.11)	8.90:1
1st (3.41)	14.39:1
Final drive ratio	4.22:1

CHASSIS & BODY

Layout	front engine/rear drive
Brake system	8.2-in. (208-mm) discs front, 7.0 x 1.1-in. (178 x 28-mm) drums rear
Wheels	wire, 14 x 4½J
Tires	steel-belted radial, 145R-14
Steering type	rack & pinion
Turns, lock-to-lock	2.2

Suspension, front/rear: unequal-length A-arms, Spax coil spring/tube shock units, anti-roll bar/live axle, dual trailing arms, Panhard rod, Spax coil spring/tube shock units

Most test cars arrive at our palatial Newport Beach offices in one of two ways. Either the manufacturer drops the car off on our doorstep or we go to the manufacturer's distribution center and pick up the car ourselves.

Very seldom does a test car arrive completely disassembled on three separate forklift pallets in the back of an airfreight delivery truck. Equally seldom does half the staff stay well past quitting time on a Friday night to greet a car and lift its various and weighty components from the back of that same truck (yes, we have no forklift). In fact, these things have never happened at all, until recently.

Blame for this sudden madness can be placed squarely on the shoulders of three people. First, the late and brilliant Colin Chapman, who in the mid-Fifties designed a lovely aerodynamic sports racing car called the Lotus 11. The second guilty party is an Englishman named Chris Smith, whose Westmidlands firm has long specialized in the restoration of vintage Lotus racing cars. It dawned on Smith that it would be just about as easy to build an entirely new Lotus 11 from the ground up as to restore some of the bent and rusted iron that came through the front door of his shop, so he set up production facilities to produce a Lotus 11 replica known as a Westfield. The third culpable individual is R&T's own English correspondent Doug Nye (curse these clever Englishmen) who wrote a glowing report about the Westfield sports car for our June 1983 issue and gave all of us a vicious dose of the dreaded English Sports Car Lust, a disease many believed had been eradicated by modern technology.

In other words, after reading Doug's article on the Westfield car, we all wanted one. Being eyeball deep in canceled checks from my Lotus 7 restoration project (talk about bent and rusted iron), I decided the cheapest solution to this craving was to con-

CRATE EXPECTATIONS

Building Westfield's Lotus 11 replica

BY PETER EGAN
PHOTOS BY THE AUTHOR

PHOTO BY BARBARA EGAN

Road & Track's sophisticated new forklift at work on arrival day.

Driver's footwell came filled with trim pieces and ancillary items.

vince the Good Editor, the Beneficent Publisher and the Kindly Business Manager that what this magazine needed was a really good kit car, to be assembled as a magazine project. It worked.

The very words "kit car," of course, may be enough to send shivers of dread up and down the spine of the average hard-core car enthusiast. They conjure up immediate images of a disreputable parody of some nice old British roadster tarted up with too much upholstery, fake louvers, the wrong steering wheel, phony exhaust plumbing, a picnic basket where the engine should be and a tell-tale set of Volkswagen mufflers whistling from beneath the rear deck. There are a few nicely done kit cars around, but most tend to misinterpret the spirit of the original classic, or cost more than the real thing. Or both.

In reading Doug Nye's report, however, a picture emerged of a nicely crafted, eminently affordable kit that stuck very close to the original design and avoided many of the usual replicar pitfalls. With its tubular steel space frame and riveted aluminum chassis panels, the Westfield is very close in design to the original 11. It differs only in the use of fiberglass for the upper body panels (molds lifted from the original Lotus aluminum), heavier-duty tubing and a few extra braces in the frame to handle the rigors of street and pothole, and a slightly lengthened cockpit section to accommodate tall drivers and the Sprite driveshaft.

Though various engines can be adapted, the basic Westfield kit is designed around that widely available junkyard phenomenon, the drivetrain from a rusted-out Sprite or Midget, preferably the 1275-cc version. A live rear axle, also Sprite, is located by a Panhard rod and four trailing links. The front suspension uses Spridget spindles, steering rack, hubs and disc brakes, but the suspension pieces are fabricated Lotus-like from steel tube. As on the original 11 (and 7) the front anti-roll bar doubles as

The Westfield sports car, laid out and ready for assembly.

the front half of the upper A-arm. Coil springs and adjustable Spax tubular shocks are used front and rear.

Like most early Lotus cars, the 11 was always available in kit form with a variety of proprietary engines, so a modern-day kit seems like an extension of—rather than an affront to—tradition. The Le Mans model was powered by the 1100 Climax engine and had De Dion rear suspension, but the more affordable Club model used a live rear axle, and the still cheaper Sports version used a live rear axle with the inexpensive side-valve Ford 100E engine. The original 11 also came either with or without the aerodynamic hump behind the driver, and Chris Smith offers the Westfield in both body styles.

The U.S. distributor for Westfield is Rev-Pro Engineering Inc in Sarasota, Florida, another restoration and racing fabrication shop, owned by a very helpful gentleman named Willard Howe. Rev-Pro (6223 S. McIntosh Rd, Sarasota, Fla. 33583; 813 922-7371) sells the cars in full or partial kits, or as completely assembled vehicles, depending upon the customers wishes and checking account. All mechanical components are reconditioned. Prices range from $4600 for a basic chassis kit sans running gear and other Sprite pieces, up to $10,500 for a fully assembled car. At the time we decided to go ahead with the project, all Rev-Pro's cars were spoken for, so we called Chris Smith in England and found that he had an unsold left-hand-drive car with blue upholstery nearly completed on the assembly line.

By the time we ordered the car I had already tracked down a really clapped-out 1971 MG Midget ($400, with crash damage and no discernible oil pressure) that I planned to rebuild for our drivetrain. Chris Smith informed us, however, that his price for a freshly rebuilt engine, transmission and rear axle was only $1100. That was less than it would have cost to buy and rebuild the innards of the $400 Midget, so we ordered the complete kit for a total cost of $7100. We requested the car be airfreighted, as I hoped to have it built in time to drive to the June Sprints at Elkhart Lake, Wisconsin. If you think it's expensive to airmail a Christmas card to your aunt in London, try sending a car. The postage figure is best left unmentioned. Take our advice and let Willard Howe get you one by boat. Have patience and it shall make you rich.

Sprite rear axle uses existing brackets for shock and trailing link installation. Only modification is stud for Panhard rod.

Three weeks after placing our order, the car was at the door. The Westfield actually arrived as three separate shipments; one for the chassis parts, one for the 1965 MG Midget engine and transmission, and the last containing the rear axle assembly. The largest pallet, of course, carried the chassis and primer-gray fiberglass bodyshell. This arrived covered with plastic wrap, criss-crossed with yellow tape reading "FRAGILE" and filled to the gunwales with random Westfield parts.

Unloading the pieces from the chassis tub was about as close to Christmas morning as anything I've experienced since the earlier part of my arrested childhood. The driver's and passenger's footwells were filled with items such as red Maserati air horns, carefully wrapped plexiglass windshield pieces, throttle and choke cables, exhaust header, red leather-covered steering wheel, a BSA motorcycle muffler, hood latches, bags of nuts and bolts and other pieces whose mysterious functions became clear only as assembly progressed.

I was surprised at the completeness and finish of the chassis when we got the miscellaneous parts cleared away. The basic chassis arrived fully painted and upholstered, with the dash (instruments mounted) and all the aluminum panels riveted in place. The front suspension was bolted loosely together, and the pedal assembly, steering rack and column were fitted. The engine, transmission, rear axle and brakes were all clean, freshly painted and—from all appearances—thoroughly reconditioned.

Not one printed word of instructional material was included with the kit, but unless you're the sort of person who accidentally bolts exhaust headers to the rear axle, the relative position of parts is pretty self-evident. The Westfield is basic automobile at its best.

14

I decided the most logical progression was to get the car on its wheels with the brakes hooked up, install the wiring harness, slide in the engine, transmission and cooling system and get the car driveable before dealing with the bodywork and cosmetics.

Assembly of the rear suspension is reasonably easy. You center the rear axle in the frame and then shim the trailing links with washers so they move freely with the axle in its proper location. With the axle shimmed the Panhard rod drops right into place and the handbrake assembly can be hooked up. Front suspension, as mentioned, was already bolted loosely together, but there was more involved than just tightening down the bolts. Because of differences in manufacturing tolerances and weld thicknesses, some of the suspension bolts were too short for correct bedding of the locking rings in the Ny-lok nuts, so I did a bit of juggling with washers and bolts, filing the surfaces and substituting with bolts from my own massive and motley collection of project leftovers (the Westfield now has a grade-8 Lola trailing link bolt holding its left lower A-arm in place).

In the never-assume-anything school of auto mechanics, I took out all the factory-assembled nuts and bolts, to inspect and reassemble them with thread locking compound. If you aren't in a hurry to get the car ready for a trip to Elkhart Lake, it is probably also a good idea to drill and safety wire some of the more crucial suspension bolts. I didn't, however, and nothing loosened up after the car was assembled and driven.

Assembling the brake system was time-consuming because the flare fittings were new and unbedded and they all leaked after the initial tightening. Some sealed after considerable loosening and retightening, and others needed burrs touched up with light emery paper. The front calipers have double pistons and were very difficult to bleed because air wants to stay trapped in them. The calipers had to be removed from the spindles and rotated at various odd angles during bleeding (with a steel spacer between the pads) to get the air out. Even now, the pedal is not quite as hard as it should be, and I suspect there's a renegade bubble in there somewhere.

I greased the hub splines and mounted the brand-new 14-in. MGB wire wheels and Ceat Veltro radials, tightened the knockoffs down with a lead hammer and lowered the car to the ground. A roller.

At the time our kit was shipped, Westfield had not completed production of its wiring looms, and part of the deal was you had to fabricate all your own wiring. Chris Smith knew we were short on time, so he kindly tossed in a stock wiring loom out of a late model MG Midget. I spent two nights going blind on wiring diagrams and trying to track down wires that led to nonexistent 4 way flashers and seatbelt buzzers before throwing the MG wiring loom at a nearby stack of empty beer cans and cigarette butts. I called two friends, John Jaeger and Roger Salter, both of whom have restored many old British cars and profess actually to *like* making up wiring looms. (Too much Guinness. Or not enough.) At any rate, they're very good at it and fabricated a beautiful harness while I used the R&T floor hoist and a chain to drop in the engine and transmission. The drivetrain went in effortlessly, once I put the motor mounts in right-side up.

I adjusted the valves, installed the distributor, set the static timing, added oil, hooked up the battery, cranked the engine for oil pressure (70 psi cold), installed the plugs and twisted the key. The engine fired immediately, settling down to a smooth, mellow idle through the BSA bike muffler. I took the car out for a midnight drive and the throttle immediately stuck wide open (minor adjustment). Otherwise the car ran, felt and sounded beautiful. Without the weight of the bodywork it felt like a go kart and accelerated like hell, almost leaping down the road under bursts of acceleration.

In its standard position, the clutch pedal had too little travel to fully disengage the clutch, so I got my welder and made an adjustable pushrod for the clutch master cylinder. Those with shorter legs could accomplish the same thing by moving the entire pedal cluster closer to the driver by drilling a few holes in the pedal support bracket.

We sent the bodywork out to a paint shop while the fine mechanical details were being looked after. I've painted at least a dozen cars myself and now have lungs I imagine to be about two thirds filled with Bondo, primer dust and paint spray, so I prefer to farm it out these days. We chose a soft white paint with a medium blue racing stripe down the middle of the car. The color was chosen partly for tradition, because R&T had a Lotus 11 in American racing colors on the cover of the March 1957 issue when we first tested the car. The other reason was because the fiberglass on the Westfield is a bit bumpy and cobby and reflects fewer of its flaws in a lighter color. A dark green, for instance, would demand a lot of sanding and preparation.

The final project was to install the windshield, doors, side windows, headlights and covers. Most of these pieces come undrilled, so careful positioning is required to make everything fit before the holes are drilled. The kit provides polished brass nuts and bolts for windshield attachment, which add a nice finishing touch. The headlight covers needed some moderate shaping on a belt sander to fit their recessed openings, and the quartz-halogen headlamps provided were too long for the headlight buckets, so we installed a pair of smaller 6-in. motorcycle headlamps under the covers. The lights and all the wiring worked, the horn honked, and the car was done.

As kit cars go, I would say the Westfield has just about the right balance. It is not so thoroughly pre-assembled that anyone can just slap it together with acceptable results, nor is it so difficult that someone with reasonable mechanical skills and a good set of tools—and plenty of spare bolts and washers—can't produce a pleasing, well finished car. That, of course, is the appeal of a kit car. No two will come out quite the same, and the car becomes an expression of the builder's patience, craftsmanship and vision. The Westfield is a sound, well designed car that holds no unpleasant surprises for its constructor, but demands just enough careful massaging and detailing to make the construction process interesting and personal. When you're done, you feel as though you own this car in a way no one else can.

Working nights and weekends, I was able to finish the project in just over three weeks with a little help from my friends. That, of course, does not include the sanding and painting of the fiberglass bodyshell, which was done by a paint shop to the tune of $600. So with the cost of our kit, the paint work, and random nuts, bolts, fittings, fluids, wire and tape, the total cost of the car (excluding airfreight) was well under $8000. Expensive, but not bad these days for a new sports car, and cheaper than many other kits and replicas on the market. A buyer could save money, of course, by purchasing the basic chassis kit and then hunting down his own drivetrain, instruments and ancillary items.

How does the car work? Just fine, thank you. It's quick, light, fun to drive, and handles so well you can't believe the suspension was designed nearly 30 years ago. (But then the man who designed it was good at this sort of thing.) Suffice it to say that when the sun is just rising on a Sunday morning and you just happen to own a cap and a pair of goggles, the Westfield is not a bad thing to have lurking in your garage.

'This is a car you'll either love or hate. If you're the kind of enthusiast willing to endure hurricane, freeze and flood in a fun car, the Westfield Seven is very appealing indeed.'

I flicked down two gears, rolled onto the brakes and drew to a halt smartly on the front row at the traffic lights. My daughter wrestled with the mini-bales of rabbit hay and straw wedged between her and the red-covered dashboard and giggled, complaining mildly that her ears were ringing. Over to the right, on the traffic island in the middle of the Farnham Bypass, an admiring group of pedestrians grinned approval – November and the hood was down.

"D'you suffer Lotus elbow?", called the most knowledgeable of them. "No" I replied, "It's the Westfield W'ist in this case…", flapping a limp hand over the side. "Good poser's car innit…"

That hadn't really occurred to me before. When Chris Smith lent me this Coventry Climax FWB-engined effective-replica of an original Series I Lotus 7, I had never dreamed it would attract so much attention. I'm not by nature a replicar fan, indeed my whole background rebels against the very thought, but when it comes to bringing fifties-style motoring squarely within the grasp of the *ordinary* enthusiast – and especially the impecunious youngster – then I believe that's something else *if*, and it's a big if, the job is nicely done.

When it is as nicely done as in Chris Smith's new Westfield Seven, then I for one am prepared to applaud the 1983 Bellini Historic Sports Car Champion's approach, wave my arms about and spread the word…

Colin Chapman described his original 7 as the "…most basic, lightest, high-performance little car – a student's car if you will – a four-wheeled motor-bike…" He unveiled it to a startled public alongside the Elite coupé at the Earls Court Motor Show of October 1957. Typically Chapman, it was based upon a sparse spaceframe, welded-up from round and square-section tube stock, with rivetted-on aluminium stiffening panels. Its independent front suspension and live-axle rear end derived from the contemporary Lotus Elite/Eleven Club thinking and the 7 was a logical extension of the old Mark 6 theme which preceded it.

Beginner's competition car

In essence the Series I was intended as a beginner's competition car in which one could learn the art of controlling a high-performance lightweight on road and track. In June 1960 it was replaced by a more refined Series II to become 'a road car also useable on circuit', and the succeeding Lotus 7s and Super 7s followed, culminating today in Caterham Cars' highly-developed and highly-entertaining fun machines.

What Chris Smith set out to do less than two years ago, when he founded Westfield Sports Cars Ltd to produce a look-alike enveloping-bodied Lotus 11 replicar, was to bring that type of motoring much

WILD WEST

Doug Nye takes to the road in Westfield's Lotus lookalike fun machine

more within reach of the man in the street – catering for the average *Autosport* or CLASSIC & SPORTSCAR reader as opposed to the high earner looking for ways to enjoy his spare cash. There were two ways to do this. One was to slap together a cut-price rolling accident looking for a likely place to happen. The other was offer a low-labour kit, to trim profit margins with a realistic pricing policy, keep overheads low and pull together a dedicated and capable workforce willing to get their heads down and beaver, hard. As an example, their welder worked regular 60-hour weeks throughout the past year!

Smith is a pretty blunt, practical character, and he explains his value-for-money pricing policy with the

Primitive – the internals of a Westfield Seven shell

line: "I want to sell 'em – not collect 'em…"

He thought he might, just, be able to sell a couple of dozen Westfield 11s over two or three years. In fact within the first year production has already exceeded 105 and orders are still rolling in. The original product has been extensively developed and improved and an eager distribution chain in the USA is already into repeat orders.

Better term than replica

Now a separate company, Westfield Seven Ltd, has been set up to handle the latest lookalike – and that's a better term than replica, for both the Eleven and the Seven are obviously different animals from the Lotus prototypes upon close inspection. An impressive feature of both Westfield models is the rigidity of their tubular spaceframe chassis. For simplicity both are welded-up from square-section stock, and while neither Lotus featured centreline framing around the transmission tunnel both Westfields have it.

Both are sold in kit form, the idea being that you invest in a rusted-out Spridget, buy the kit and then assemble it to use reconditioned engine, gearbox, braking system, axle and so on, cannibalised from the Sprite or Midget. Smith would prefer not to become involved in total assembly to sell finished cars, but it can be arranged. He does provide a service to perform any small specialist operations the kit builder might find problematic, and in addition the Eleven is available in various degrees of kit-completion. That does not apply to the Seven, however, the new kit for which is available in one specification only, priced at £2750 plus VAT. In theory, with a £2-300 outlay on a scrap Spridget you can put your self-built fun car on the road for something the right side of £3500-£3750. And there's not a lot of worthwhile choice available when it comes to performance cars around that mark.

The basic kit is not as comprehensive as one might expect of something like the Caterham Seven, which includes all mechanical parts, but it takes in the following items: Aluminium-panelled epoxy-powder coated chassis frame in grey or black finish with bright panelling, ready-fitted with scuttle, bonnet dash and glass-fibre nose cone; self-coloured glass-fibre wings with all necessary brackets; laminated windscreen with two side brackets; hood and hoodframe; five-gallon aluminium fuel tank; four front suspension wishbones; four rear trailing arms; one rear Panhard rod with all relevant suspension bushes; two Panhard rod location brackets for welding onto the Spridget back axle (the company will do this for the customer if he brings the axle in, or will supply part-exchange overseas); pair of rear wheel spacers to give chassis clearance; steering wheel and column including UJs; complete wiring loom; two Lotus 7 Series I-style Butler tractor headlamps; two Austin A35 side-lights; four indicator lamps; upholstered cockpit seat back and two squabs; four adjustable Spax dampers and coil-springs, and an original-style exhaust manifold and silencer – the silencer actually being a Peugeot estate rear box...

This standard Seven kit is jigged entirely for Spridget parts, but a special-engined alternative for rather more than twice the kit price would be 1460cc Coventry Climax FWB-engined like the prototype car loaned to me for test.

Before describing that device, I should explain the fundamental differences between the Westfield Seven and the Lotus prototype on which it is based, for while it retains the low-sprung pert looks of the 1957 original it embodies numerous improvements.

For a start it is 3ins longer to give more cockpit room, though the nose, bonnet and scuttle all fit an original Series I. The cockpit shoulder room is also 1in greater than an original 'S1', 39ins instead of 38. The Westfield has that hefty tunnel framing for added rigidity in all planes. Where the Lotus rear axle was located by an A-frame beneath the diff-casing and twin trailing arms, the Westfield has four trailing arms and a lateral Panhard rod. This is because the original-style A-arm tended to twist the axle casing and could snap off the lug under the diff. This caused oil leaks which proved a classic 7 ailment.

The Lotus' front suspension used a front-mounted, high anti-roll bar sweeping back to couple-up with lateral links forming the top wishbones. The Westfield has no anti-roll bar, but proper wishbones. The Lotus' original rear coil-springs had axial-pin top location. This pin tended to rust-up, locking-on the fixing nuts. The Westfield's Spax dampers locate on a horizontal through-bolt fixing instead. Its Midget-derived handbrake rising from the passenger side of the transmission tunnel is also more efficient than the original under-dash device. Whereas the Lotus drew its component parts from a variety of off-the-shelf sources, the Westfield uses just one, the Austin-Healey Sprite/MG Midget range.

So what's it like?

Dependent on your outlook, this is a car you'll either love or hate. You'll know the moment you see the photos here whether it attracts you or not, and that means whether you are the kind of enthusiast willing to endure hurricane, freeze and flood in a fun car – or want more civilisation for your money. If this kind of car appeals at all, then Westfield's Seven 'Series I look-alike' is very appealing indeed.

The test car had an extra attraction for me as it was fitted with a 1460cc Coventry Climax FWB engine. This 4-cylinder sohc all-alloy unit is the kind upon which Lotus and Cooper built their reputation in sports and Formula 2 racing in the late 'fifties. It's entirely in keeping with the Seven, and makes it a mouth-watering cut above the Spridget-engined basic model. That also makes it more expensive, with the engine costing more than the rest of the car.

Probably become his test chassis

Tony Mantle of Climax Engine Services built and owned 'my' FWB, and this particular Westfield Seven will probably become his test chassis. He is a one-man band who maintains and services all the best Climax engines, including that used in Nigel Sheffield's Lotus 17 which Chris Smith drove to the Bellini Championship this past season for Sheffield Garner Ltd, the Ford main agents from Diss, Norfolk.

There is an ulterior motive for the Seven-Climax, in that if sufficient demand can be created for Climax-engined variants it could allow a fair-sized production batch of suitable units to be set up, in turn minimising their individual cost. This could be a two-edged sword, however, for Tony works alone, has built around 30 engines in the past year and finds that workload sufficient. He'd have to take on and train staff to handle more, so he's more inclined to keep unit price quite high and supply a restricted demand. As things stand at the moment he's quoting "not less than £3000" for an FWB engine similar to the one in the Seven test car. On balance I have to say that seems worthwhile, for around £6500 you have a near-genuine throw-back to 'fifties

Evocative – the Westfield Seven has all the right looks

Delectable – two Westfield Lotus 11 lookalikes line up

motoring, with all the right looks, sensations, sounds ... and drawbacks. And that's half the fun.

In Seven trim the FWB breathes through twin SU 1½-inch carburettors and with a compression ratio around 9.5:1 and a mild road-going camshaft is believed to give some 85bhp ... plus considerable mid-range torque. It drives via a standard Spridget gearbox with that notchy but surprisingly rapid change, and non-synchro first gear. For competition, bottom gear proved notoriously weak in this 'box, but I didn't know that until too late ...

The Seven cockpit is surprisingly roomy, despite that square-edged panelled-in transmission tunnel with its extra longitudinal frame tubes. I'm around 5ft 11ins tall and my feet could barely reach the pedals. It's better to have too-long a cockpit and cushion short drivers forward, than to have one too short and cramp taller men. I put the passenger seat squab behind my back which proved more comfortable than it sounds, and it did the trick.

Finish on the Westfield is generally very good, though one or two ragged corners will have to be improved on the aluminium scuttle panelling, and the glass-fibre wing mouldings showed minor imperfections. Smith's Elevens are already onto their third set of ever-improving body moulds, and I would expect Seven development to follow suit. He acts upon criticism.

Access with the well-made heavy-gauge hood erected is like making love to the circus fat lady.

Super – Climax FWB twin carb engine turns out some 85bhp

Where d'you begin? The answer is either to give up before you start, furl the hood and tuck it away in the unfloored space behind the cockpit, above the fuel tank, or to step in head first, bring in the trailing foot thereafter, turn around with your head bulging-out the hood, and then slither legs down into the footwell. From outside it looks hilarious, with the hood stretching and heaving in all directions, wife leaning helpless with laughter against the garage door. I took the hood down, and the weatherman smiled upon us with a spell of mild, dry weather.

The Climax engine starts easily with a deafening blast from the out-turned side exhaust, blowing-up dead leaves three or four yards away.

The Westfield Seven inherits the stiffness and fine ride quality of its Eleven predecessor. Even at speed on quite rough country roads only those tall-bracketed tractor headlights shimmy noticeably, and the chassis/body structure proves remarkably rigid. It also runs arrow-straight hands-off in those conditions, while the soft-sprung/stiff-damped suspension with low tyre pressures soak up ridges and bumps remarkably well.

In finest Lotus tradition

Steering is high-geared and direct in the finest Lotus tradition. With the wheels in sight you can aim the car very accurately indeed. Brakes which are perhaps no more than adequate on the standard Spridget are quite powerful without being fierce and prone to grabbing in the lightweight Seven. In normal driving, off the mark acceleration was certainly vivid, the tacho needle whacking round to the 6000rpm 'caution' mark most impressively through the gears. I didn't manage to take proper times but 0-60 *felt* like something in the 7secs bracket.

To preserve original looks and proportions, Chris supplied the car with 15in MGA wire wheels carrying narrow-tread 155 SR-15 tyres front and rear on 4J and 4½J rims. In this form the Seven was prone to wagging its tail, especially in roundabouts and tight corners and it was obvious the FWB gave just too much power for the contact patch available. On wider 165 SR 15s behaviour was improved. Now you could kick the tail out and within reason hold it there, the rigid frame giving a great feeling of stable security. With more grippy tyres than those Kelly-Springfields perhaps it would all feel better still. . . there was more juggling to be done and I was enjoying myself heartily charging around the Hampshire byways. Eventually I decided the time had come to try some standing starts.

Tacho needle vertical, 3500rpm, seemed a reasonable place to start, so with the FWB singing lustily away I snicked-in first, checked the mirror, and popped the clutch.

An earthquake struck, the poor little Seven bounded into the air and clattered to rest, and I switched off, wondering what on earth I had done.

It was remarkable, visible testimony to the FWB's torque. The lower radius rods either side are quite short, made of 16-gauge steel tube; heavy, thick and virtually impossible to bend even in a vice. Now they had bent through some 45-degrees, the left-side tube down until it bottomed-out against the chassis lower rail and the right-side tube upwards, the axle twisting bottom forwards as those Kelly-Springfield rear tyres refused to break traction and spin! As the left-side radius rod bottomed-out on the chassis rail – and the prop-shaft UJ on the side of the transmission tunnel – the axle could rotate no further, so that weak bottom gear stripped.

I didn't feel very proud of myself, but they had asked me to test the prototype. If you can't take a joke, you shouldn't have joined. In fact a redesign is under way, and you can be sure a better car will emerge. Remember I was impressed by it as it stood.

Chris Smith has set out to bring this type of classical Lotus motoring within reach of Mr Average, and is doing the job very well. For around £3500 and the investment of some hours' sweat you can be on the road in a well-made, robust and well-thought out classical style performance car – destruction-tested by experts in this case ... Some years ago after testing a Caterham Seven – which is in a higher price bracket – I wrote that it was hard to believe so much fun could be legal. That holds true today.

GHG 685F

Seventh Son

It may not have passed without notice, but there is more than one car that looks like a Lotus. Three, in fact: the original Lotus Seven, Caterham's current Seven and now the Westfield Seven, plus many others on the same theme — but nothing near like so detailed. The link between the Seven that Lotus made and the car that Caterham now produce is far from tenuous.

Caterham took over the rights to produce the Seven when Lotus were moving upmarket and rationalising their production racing car side, which made Sevens in the spare time. The car that was in production at the time was the boxy Seven series four, from which the Dutton took so much inspiration. But potential Seven owners had demonstrated — by paying a lot of money for the older models — that what they really wanted was its forerunner, the series three, which stuck far closer to the original theme and was a positive wild horse when it had a Lotus Elan-style twin-cam engine installed. That's the basis of today's Caterham Seven with mild or wild power units.

Now, although the appearance of the Seven series three was similar to that of every other Lotus of the same type, it had developed quite a lot along the line from the time it was a series one in 1957. And Chris Smith's latest offering — remember his glorious Lotus Eleven lookalike, the Westfield Eleven, in our issue of February 1983? — is, in reality, a Lotus Seven series one with some mods of his own. You might think that Caterham would be upset, but demand is high for their Seven, and then you realise, when you drive first a Caterham Seven, and then the Westfield Seven, that, draughts apart, they are quite different cars.

The Caterham Seven, when powered by around 115bhp of twin-cam, like a friend's X-registered example in which I have travelled at a considerable rate of knots, is a very rapid motor car, up to the 80s; then like all such square-cut projectiles, its aerodynamics — which have been likened to those of a brick — start to work against further progress. By the time it has touched 100mph, you get the feeling that it wouldn't matter how much power you had, it wouldn't go much faster; it would just get there a bit quicker, which is all very well on the track, but if you think about it, you'd have a hard time using any more acceleration on the road! You'd be forever squirting, then squirming out of the way of people who never guessed you close up on them so fast. And the suspension has to be quite stiff to cope with such, well, wild horse, performance.

It was with these thoughts in mind that Chris Smith designed a quite different car. He stuck to his spaceframe principles, developed as long as 15 years ago when he built the first of the spaceframe Spridgets that were so fast they got the rules of Modsports changed to give other people a chance. These new rules meant that you couldn't remove any metal from within the wheelbase, which suddenly made the Lotus Elan one of the most competitive things imaginable because it didn't have much metal there to start with thanks to its lightweight backbone frame. So Chris got into Lotuses and subsequently campaigning the Lotus Eleven's ultimate development, the tiny Lotus 17, to great effect in historic racing.

Now it may not have passed without notice, but quite a lot of historic cars are bogus. The mechanical parts have been changed what seems a million times, the body panels no end of times, and the chassis several times, or they might never have been more than a pile of spare parts, but they are still hailed as the original car! Chris has never been involved in this trade, but he knew well how much it cost to retain original parts from his business restoring old racing cars. So when a client asked him how much it would cost to refurbish a rusting wreck of a Lotus Eleven frame and make it into a road car, Chris said it would be cheaper and better to build a new one. Now, the original Coventry-Climax mechanics are scarce and expensive, but, at that time, in 1982, old Spridgets were thick under foot. So, with his Modsport days in mind, Chris built his customer a replica Lotus Eleven, using MG Midget running gear — but being a straightforward and honest guy, he didn't call it a Lotus:

Engine bay with the standard Spridget power unit, leaving room to reach everything with the utmost ease . . . and to dream of what else you could put in there.

he named it after his home, Westfield House.

Some 100 Westfields later, Chris caught up with himself: within a year, he had established a network of agents all over the world, selling Westfield Elevens almost as fast as he could make them, with a variety of power units (Honda for emission-conscious Japan, Datsun on the way for the land of Plenty Old Bluebirds, the USA). The supply of old Spridgets was turning out to be not all that great, as people restored them. So, today, most of Chris's Westfields are supplied with brand-new British Leyland parts to complement their excellent workmanship. But there was one problem: the highly aerodynamic, and rather bulbous, bodywork of the Eleven was not really suitable for everyday use. Like the Lotus Eleven of old, it was

Long glove-fit cockpit of the Westfield features special Chris Smith Lotus-like steering wheel, Spridget mechanicals and instruments, Lotus replica screen (aero screens optional).

really a racing car that could be used on the road, and like Lotus in the late 1950s, Chris saw a market for a road-going version, the Seven series one.

It's made just like the Eleven, with 16swg square and round tubing, strong enough to stand any shocks the road can dole out (which is more than you can say for the original Eleven), plus stressed aluminium panelling, including the transmission tunnel. Colin Chapman hardly ever made a car for anybody taller than himself, and he was only 5ft 8in; so Chris — who is 6ft 2in — made the cockpit of his Eleven wider to give more room to wriggle in for those broader in the beam and longer in the leg. But there was a problem in this aspect with the Seven because the body had to stay fairly narrow, not only for the sake of appearance, but for ultimate handling in the wet and to fit in with a standard British Leyland Spridget back axle. So the Westfield Seven, which is build on a quite different jig at his works in Netherton, West Midlands, has a longer wheelbase, by three inches.

It is this point, allied with a far softer coil spring/adjustable damper suspension all round, that helps make the Westfield feel so much different to the Caterham. It weighs only 1375lb with its alloy and glassfibre bodywork — 200lb lighter than a Spridget — but rides even better. The Caterham, on the other hand, reminds you of every ripple in the road. The steering is the same, delightfully light and accurate rack and pinion, but I'd say that a Caterham would have a hard time cornering as fast as a Westfield on give-and-take, twisting, bumpy, roads. But then you'd have to swap dampers and springs — a 20min job — to make the Westfield fully competitive for the track.

With only 65bhp from a standard Spridget unit, the acceleration is not in the same league as that of the Caterham, but it was still as fast as an XR3, I discovered; and the Westfield is every bit as nimble as machines like the Chevette and Fiesta that have taken over as the sports cars for the masses — plus the blast of fresh air that the Spridget had as its great bonus. On 65bhp, top speed is limited to 85mph, but then so is the price of the basic kit limited to £1595 plus VAT and the mechanical parts — and engine and gearbox, rear axle and steering. But, then, you have only to look at the size of the engine bay to see how much room there is for any reasonably narrow power unit of similar weight . . . or any of the masses of

tuning gear available for the A-Series engine.

A day in the Westfield made me realise what an ideal car it is for any sporting occasion, especially an autotest, provided you can put up with so much fresh air. Even with the sketchy hood erect, you've got to be tough to drive it in the winter . . . but wasn't that always the way with open cars or cars without a heater? ●

Fabricated wishbone front suspension takes in Spridget uprights and steering rack, plus easily adjusted or changed coil spring/damper units.

Westfield frames are made on a jig and then panelled in aluminium for extra rigidity.

Westfield Sports Cars

Latter-day Lotuses?

AT A SMALL industrial estate in Dudley, West Midlands, the observant passer-by who glances into a small, neat, factory unit may be surprised to see what is apparently a congregation of Lotus X1s and 7s. Apparently, because closer scrutiny will reveal that most of them bear a small badge which says "Westfield", rather than the circular yellow sign of Colin Chapman. At a time when "replicas" of one sort or another proliferate, this may seem upsetting to supporters of the marque. Yet the man who has brought this project into being is a devoted Lotus fan himself.

Chris Smith has been racing his own Lotuses for some years, and is currently campaigning a 17 in Historic racing, with which he won last year's Bellini Championship outright. Having learned to maintain and repair his cars by hard experience, he agreed to a friend's request to build a new Lotus X1 chassis from scratch. In the event he built two, and when the first appeared in a magazine article clad in a GRP body which was indistinguishable from the original, the response was enthusiastic enough to prompt him to go into full-time production. That was in 1982; last year the X1 was joined by a 7-lookalike based on the same mechanicals, although the latter, of

course, is in a rather different light since the original model is effectively still in production under the Caterham name. (In order to minimise any obvious comparison the Westfield 7 utilises the cycle-type front mudguards of earlier Lotuses rather than the flared wings which succeeded them.) The two models have been a surprising success — during 1983, 110 cars were delivered, of which a high proportion were sent across the Atlantic. Most of these sales were in kit form, in which case the purchaser provides certain components himself, these being from the MG Midget, namely the engine / gearbox, propshaft, rear axle, steering column and brakes. Despite this re-use of proprietary components, Smith is at pains to distance himself from the "kit-car" image, pointing out that what he is producing now is very similar to what Chapman offered originally. In fact, he claims, his cars offer improvements over the originals in certain areas, such as replacing the riveted alloy transmission tunnel with a steel tube tunnel.

In other respects, the chassis are perfect copies of Chapman's designs, although built in square steel tubing rather than round, and under the GRP body are clad in aluminium panelling of very high quality, all of which is carried out by Smith's own workforce.

The simplicity of the cars and the kit option means that the price is very low — £2,750 for the 7, and only £2,268 for even the most complete version of the X1 kit. This means that a purchaser could build a complete running vehicle for £3,000.

Perhaps surprisingly, therefore, Westfield's customer does not tend to be the impecunious young car enthusiast, but is more likely to be someone who remembers the Lotus X1 in its heyday, someone who has always wanted to own the real thing, or who perhaps did and now regrets selling it. Up until this year, the only opportunity to enjoy such a car was the occasional afternoon spin on a warm day, since there is of course no weather protection, but in 1984 a new option presents itself. The 750 Motor Club, for long the stalwarts in low-cost racing, are organising a race category which will accept replicas, and here the Westfield should be a popular choice.

Construction

The steel tube chassis, as previously described, is panelled internally in aluminium, and mounts fabricated wishbones at the front, and trailing arms at the rear. The Midget axle is modified to accept coil-spring units, and a steel fuel tank

THE all-alloy Climax unit with twin SUs installed in the 7.

21

sits behind the engine, filled via a large alloy filler-cap.

Clothing all this is the sweeping form of Chapman's body design, executed flawlessly in GRP, complete with a very low wraparound screen. A raised headrest with fairing is available as an option. The entire nose and tail sections can be removed, which makes for very easy access not only to the engine, but also to the suspension. As on the original, the thick, shallow doors let down like drawbridges once the small clips holding the top edges of the screen together are undone, but it is debatable whether access is any easier this way than by stepping over the closed doors. Sliding down inside reveals that there is surprisingly little legroom, leaving a lot of pilot exposed to the slipstream. The level of trim is up to the

buyer; the X1 that we photographed just before it was shipped to Canada was fully trimmed with bound carpet and leather, and managed to exude an air of luxury despite the basic simplicity of the dashboard and cockpit.

Naturally the performance with a Midget engine does not compare with the racing version, but the light weight of the complete car combined with the proximity of the ground and the tarmac rushing past the screen add a tremendous veneer of speed to what is actually quite respectable acceleration. As to the handling, Smith claims from his own experience that it is "probably slightly better than the early solid-axle Lotus, but not quite as good as the later cars with IRS".

As it seemed a little unfair to experiment

CLASSIC LINES — the smooth all-enveloping body of the X1.

on a wet day with the gleaming metallic green X1 just before it was prepared for its sea voyage, we settled for trying a 7 and immediately came up against a snag — there was nowhere for MOTOR SPORT'S photographer to put his camera equipment. It really is a car for driving, not for transport. Easier to slide into than the X1, it also has a great deal of legroom; in fact, the legs are fully extended along the floor, with only a thin seat cushion under the driver. This car had only the standard Midget engine, compared to the much quicker car we were loaned later on, but it served as an introduction to the sharp responses and skippy ride. The thin-rimmed wheel is comfortably close to the chest, and the slick-acting gearlever is perfectly placed, although as usual on this type of car, the handbrake is tucked under the driver's leg. It is easy to drive, pulling in any gear, and reacting quickly to the mildest twitches of the wheel, something the driver comes to appreciate after bouncing through the first few potholes. It is not that the ride is hard, just that suspension travel is limited, so that the rear tends to hop a little on its skinny 4½ in. wheels. However, it is so predictable and easy to catch that one soon begins to wish for a more powerful engine. Thus we were glad to be offered the loan of a 7 equipped with a Coventry Climax power-unit.

A HIGH level of trim is available for those cars which will spend more time on the road than the track.

Power to Spare

This all alloy block was tremendously successful in racing of all classes in the late 50s and early 60s and it is surprising to learn that you can order your Westfield with one of these engines installed — but beware, the engine is worth more than the car. That in our test car displaced 1,220 cc and produced something like 86 bhp, together with a glorious snarl from the exhaust that kept one's foot to the floor even in some very unsuitable places.

The seemingly endless urge of this engine and the very effective braking of the Midget discs made the 7 a real pleasure to squirt through winding roads, one elbow protruding vintage style from the narrow cockpit, and even at high motorway speeds the excitement outweighed the buffeting. Handling tends to the oversteer side of the equation, especially on wet surfaces when the limited traction of the thin lightly-loaded tyres allows opposite look at relatively low speeds. It is wet weather, of course, which shows up the worst problems of running a basic car like this. With no side-screens, it fills with water even standing still with the hood up; on the move it is easy to see why Lotus changed to flared wings, as water and muck are deposited in the cockpit in a gentle stream by the front wheels. The tiny wipers clear a space just big enough to peer through, and if you wear glasses your problems are multiplied by the spray that settles on them. . . .

Obviously it would be sensible to wait for a sunny day to enjoy the undoubted pleasures of this car, but British weather being what it is, it is wise to carry the detachable hood too, which brings us back to the complete lack of storage. The space behind the seats is quite open, with the axle and 5-gallon petrol tank exposed to view, whereas even a shallow shelf here would make all the difference.

Only the nosecone and mudguards of the Westfield 7 are of GRP, the rest being aluminium, including the bonnet, which lifts off once four catches have been released, and under which nestles the gleaming block and twin SUs of this remarkably tractable engine. There is no fan, and when a rush-hour traffic journey proved inevitable, the temperature rose swiftly, but fell quickly as soon as the lights changed to green.

As a pure fun car, either Westfield must be good value, combining a very stiff frame with simple components and good handling, yet somehow the 7 does not quite have enough style to offset its impracticalities. The Westfield X1, on the other hand, may be usable on even fewer days, but each of those days will be an event to be savoured.

G.C.

Westfield *looked for a design that was practical and eye-catching and came up with this Sports 2000-like prototype. Unusually, the car is designed*

RACER FOR THE ROAD

Westfield has a strong racing heritage and has now diversified into producing a street legal racer in kit form. Doug Nye visited the factory and drove the car

Kit cars tend very much to be an acquired taste. The Mark I kit-car enthusiast tends to have a literally hairy image, not quite a *Sun* reader, but I expect you follow my drift . . . Kit cars themselves tend to range from the downright crude and ugly to the bizarre; often dubiously engineered, hardly the thing to which any reasonable chap would entrust his loved ones.

But having said that, and believing it, there are some exceptions, one being those cars produced under the Westfield name by former Chevron long-distance racing driver, and more recently historic Lotus pedaller, Chris Smith.

He began manufacturing what was effectively a Lotus Eleven lookalike — although the two cars are actually as different as chalk from cheese under the skin — three years ago in Dudley. His very well-developed grp-bodied Westfield IIs won a ready market, and in two full racing seasons have become the backbone of Britain's 'kit-car' club-racing formula, dominating the class championships.

Smith figured initially that he might be able to sell a couple of dozen cars over the two years, but Westfield quality and back-up were sufficient to generate much wider demand, and several times that number were produced in the first 12 months. He then diversified to build other cars in both kit or fully-assembled export form, and Westfield Sports Cars Ltd also undertook 'real car' restoration and multi-tubular spaceframe chassis fabrication.

For some time Smith had thought about building a more modern-looking road-going sports car, and through last summer his ideas crystallised around 'something like' the Chevron B19s and Lola T210s which dominated the 2-litre European Championship sports-racing series of 1970-71. Where enthusiasts now in their late-30s or 40s might recall the front-engined Lotuses and Lolas of their youth as the prettiest proper sports cars around, for many younger enthusiasts those early '70s mid-engined 2-litre cars are the bees-knees.

Consequently, Smith and his right-hand man, welder Jack Bouckley, have now produced their new kit-built sports model, intended as a mid-engined sports-racing lookalike but actually capable of accepting either front or rear-mounted engines, in both cases driving to the rear wheels. To accumulate test mileage the first prototype has a crisp Lotus-Ford twin-cam engine and gearbox installed up front, driving to an Escort Mark I live rear axle.

Since the conventional mid-engined layout using an expensive Hewland transaxle would be prohibitively expensive, Smith decided to use instead the flat-four Alfasud power pack with its matching longitudinal gearbox-cum-final drive and inboard disc brakes acting through the driveshaft outputs. In the late lamented 'Sud' this up-to-105bhp power-pack resided ahead of the front axle line, its transaxle extending rearwards. In the latest Westfield prototype the Alfa assembly would simply be moved back in the chassis to fit ahead of the rear-axle line, aft of the cockpit, with a reversed gear-change linkage running backwards rather than forwards from the centre-line cockpit lever.

The Alfasuds did not have a good anti-rust reputation, which was bad news for used 'Sud' owners but great for today's kit-builders, because rusted-out models with still-healthy relatively low-mileage mechanicals are cheap and easily available.

Smith wanted to produce a body shape which would appeal to his potential market, and drew what you see here around an 88-inch wheelbase with obvious CanAm Chaparral, Porsche 917/10, Chevron, and Lola connotations. Out on the open road it looks low and racy, whereas in a ▶

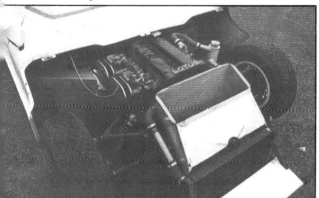

...her front or rear engines, with rear-wheel drive

Prototype *cockpit was unfinished and a little on the cramped side*

...or testing the prototype has Lotus twin-cam engine and gearbox

Nose moulding *is one piece with integrated pop-up headlamps*

Prototype *features a token windscreen although full weather equipment is being developed, as are tail fins to support a rear wing*

race paddock beside Sports 2000 cars it looks incredibly tall and hefty, with its legal-height headlamps dictating body depth. There's a bolt-on behind-the-cockpit roll-over bar included in the kit, and 'Batmobile' rear wing fins supporting a lateral spoiler will be included in the final specification with the extrovert in mind . . .

In its short life, Westfield as a marque has attracted a very loyal and enthusiastic band of supporters and customers.

What has made the Westfield 11s so effective is their very robust and rigid square-tube chassis frame, which derives much of its strength from a four-tube centre backbone with extensively cross-braced outriggers on each side. The latest sports-prototype uses a broadly similar frame, in which the deep door cut-outs each side make the backbone structure's depth and strength critical.

Last year reigning kit-car champion Robin Atkinson discovered just how strong this kind of frame is when he became over-optimistic in his Westfield 11 at Donington Park and entered a corner impossibly fast. So fast, in fact, that his car cleared the sand trap and hit the concrete wall nearly head-on. Yet he escaped with a bumped knee, while only the 11's front bay carrying the suspension folded up on impact. One lower bay tube was actually trebled into a closed-up S-bend, but every weld there held firm, none parted.

Back in the Westfield works, the crushed front bay was amputated, the frame put back on the jig and found to be undistorted, and with a new front bay welded on, the car was back out with Atkinson racing again the following weekend . . .

In the new prototype this strong frame is welded up from square-section ¾, 1 and 1½-ins mild-steel tube. Front suspension is independent, of course, using Westfield double wishbones with co-axial coil-spring dampers and Alford & Adler Triumph Spitfire uprights, disc brakes and steering. At the rear, while the front-engined prototype uses that Escort live axle carefully located by a four-link and Panhard rod system, the Alfasud mid-engined version would use Westfield coil-and-wishbone IRS.

Smith and Bouckley are a matched pair of quick-working practicians, and Westfield developments take place remarkably quickly considering their thoroughness. The new prototype's body plug was mocked up upon a 12ft by 4ft plywood sheet, on to which 13ins wheels were drawn on an 88ins wheelbase and the body line then drawn around them with a felt-tip pen. John and Charlie Cooper would have been proud of it!

Bouckley then welded up two exact copies of the outline shape in 1-inch tube, followed by two more 3ins smaller, and this smaller pair were then outrigged 3ins from the masters to provide a 3ins radius top body edge. Intermediates, cross-members and the centre backbone were drawn and welded-in, uniting all necessary

Doug Nye *listens to advice on driving technique from Chris Smith*

Versatile frame *will accommodate any four-cylinder power unit*

pick-ups and strong points, while the original body plug was hacked about and modified in Westfield's large new Kingswinford factory (and in the car park outside) until it represented what its creators felt was the right balance between practical good sense and kit-car market poseur-attraction.

You'll probably either love the result, or hate it . . . depending upon your attitude to the genre. The pair also toyed with a Group C-style full windscreen — actually from a Ferrari 512S — and fixed roof to see how a coupé would look. It seemed quite attractive and this is another available option.

Now, on one of the winter's darkest days, with the photographer spitting blood as his lightmeter advised him merely to 'go 'ome', we found Westfield's Kingswinford plant, with

Alloy wheels *are 13ins diameter*

an £80 Alfasud, severely moth-eaten but very sound mechanically, lying outside ready for the cannibals' cooking pot . . .

Excellent value has always been Smith's aim, and basically the new Westfield prototype plot is for the enthusiast owner to arm himself with just such an Alfasud, then pay £2495 (VAT extra) for the basic Westfield kit.

This includes a complete powder-coated spaceframe chassis, plus suspension, pedals, bracketry, a six-gallon fuel tank and moulded grp body self-coloured to order. This comprises one-piece nose and tail panels with inserted access hatches and integrated tail lights, vestigial prototype windscreen and two boxed door mouldings, two bucket seats, and the bolt on detachable roll-over bar.

The customer then has to fit his engine, gearbox, rear axle — if required — front uprights, steering, instruments and seat harness, for which chassis mountings are provided. Although tailored initially to either Lotus-Ford twin-cam front engine or Alfasud mid-engine, the frame will accept any conventional 4-cylinder and Westfield will modify it accordingly and supply relevant wishbones and rear trailing arms to suit whatever spec the customer requires. Of course, it would be possible to fit an Alfasud engine in each end to form a twin-engined 3-litre with four-wheel drive, but I get the impression this would be positively discouraged.

Westfield operates a sensible customer back-up and support service to help if the kit-builder loses his way. Some do, many don't, but those who do have not just been abandoned in the traditional kit-industry manner . . .

Smith believes the basic kit could be completed by a reasonably practical chap for another £500, while for £1500 he could do a really de luxe job and produce a very well-equipped and potent performer. And these days a new sports car for under £5000 tax-paid can't be bad, can it?

I drove the prototype over some viciously slippery country roads to Halfpenny Green aerodrome for a brief run and photography. First impression as I slipped into the comfortable but rather cramped and still-unfinished cockpit was that unlike my first Westfield experience with the well sorted-out 11 there was still some work to be done here.

The front engine forces the pedals rather close, but the gearbox is nicely to hand. On the rough roads to Halfpenny Green, Smith's preference for relatively long-travel soft springing but firm damping shone again. Like the 11, ride is very comfortable and well-controlled, and with the tyres faithfully following the road surface you have good traction and sufficient cornering grip — despite the slick conditions that we encountered that day.

That old half-forgotten Lotus-Ford twin-cam's crisp power impressed, like meeting an old friend again after years apart, and it pulled like a

train but ran out of revs too soon due to the stop-gap back-axle fitted. But the car is so light — only 10cwt — that it accelerated like a rocket when it wasn't spinning its relatively lightly-laden rear wheels on the frosty mud where tractors had used the lanes. And it literally took my breath clean away.

I sprouted too high above that brief screen, and above 40mph found myself drowning in the airstream. By scrunching down I could at least breathe, and forward vision remained excellent while slithering around the slick country lanes proved great — and surprisingly comfortable — fun.

Just like earlier Westfields I had experienced this is a very nicely balanced little car, obviously rigid and its handling forgiving. Of course its weight distribution would be changed with the rear engine mounting, but proportionally there would be little difference, front and rear engine mountings being well within the wheelbase.

Steering is light, direct and as full as one would expect, and although the combination of bitter weather and balding head caused me *intense* pain before the afternoon was out, I really had a lot of fun. There's still work to be done on finish, fixtures, and fittings, but the foundation of another solid Westfield fun car offering competent practical design and construction, plus excellent value for money, has been laid.

How long before the new car makes its track appearance? ■

Huge demand *was created by the early Lotus lookalike Westfields and a handful of these now dominate the kit car racing series*

7up

Following the wrangle with Caterham Cars, Westfield's old Seven has re-emerged as the SEI, with independent rear suspension. The new car is a fine antidote to '80s motoring. By Chris Harvey

THERE ARE DAYS IN A TIN TOP when you're dying to feel a fresh breeze through the hair. There are moments, too, when you want to be far from the madding motorway, and times when you need to be alone, working with your hands. Don't worry, there's an answer to all this: a car you can build yourself from a starting price of £925 that will leave the traps level with many a Porsche.

Examine the new Westfield closely and it looks desperately low-tech. Spartan is too soft a word for a car with a bench seat less than 2ins thick that you can't adjust, a saucer-sized steering wheel and tumbler switches which were old hat in 1958. But there's an answer to this, too: drive it.

Squirm into the SEI — so-called because, glory be, it is a Special Equipment model with independent rear suspension — then let your hips slide forward until your left foot finds the clutch pedal. Surprise yourself by finding that there's footroom aplenty. There never used to be in the Lotus 7 that began the crop of kit cars. Switch on the ignition, tap the accelerator three times for luck, twist the key again and savour the sound of a Formula Ford 1600 engine.

Pinch the tiny gearknob between your forefinger and thumb, flick the lever forward a couple of inches, drop the clutch and, if you get it right, you're heading for a tyre-smoking 60mph in something like 6secs. Sounds good? In the good old Westfield it used to feel bad as you bounced around like a table tennis ball — but that was a Lotus 7 clone with a live rear axle.

Racing driver Chris Smith's Westfield Sports Car company — producing 14 kit cars a week at Kingswinford, West Yorkshire — still makes an SE with a cart axle for the really hard-up. That's the £925 model. But for an extra £550 you can have the infinitely-better SEI with double wishbone-and-coil rear suspension straight from everybody else's '60s and '70s racing car.

Paste the SEI along a potholed country lane and it soaks away the bumps, storming up to 70mph. Few people will want to go faster in a car with the aerodynamics of a bath tub, although goggles and a flying helmet might see you past 100mph. But who cares? You can have more fun in a Westfield SEI at 60mph than you can at 100 in a hot hatchback. The SEI, and its close cousin, the Caterham 7, have to be the safest way to have fun on the roads without endangering your licence or anybody else.

Smith's suspension work has also improved the steering beyond the wildest dreams of kit-car drivers. Gone is the old go-kart flick, where the nose twitched from side to side as the chassis seemed to pivot somewhere around the rear axle. It has to be admitted that 185/13 Avon Turbospeeds on 6J BBS lookalike alloy wheels work wonders, but now you can power your way smoothly around long sweeping bends rather than having to follow the pattern of a 50p piece. The only real limitation of this polished performer is inherent with having to sit with your backside only 6ins from the road and head hardly higher than 3ft: the lack of visibility that comes with every verge looking like a hedge.

SEI's performance varies with the engine you choose. Smith's demonstrator has one of the old four-cylinder in-line Kent engines that used to grace Ford's pre-1981 Escort and most Cortinas, with its attendant transmission. The engine has stayed in production chiefly for Formula Ford racing. In this case, prepared by leading tuner Hugh Chamberlain, it produces 110bhp at the flywheel on twin 40DCOE Weber carburettors.

Engines like this can be bought new for around £1000 with alternatives varying between £30 for scrapyard specials — any Ford 1100cc, 1300cc, 1600cc or Lotus Twin Cam unit fits — to £6000 for a 210bhp, 1840cc unit from firms like Nick Mason Engineering.

These demon pushrod engines can work better than twin cams in cars like the Westfield because they are lighter: Mason's £1000 special, with 155bhp from 1760cc, rivals a Lotus Twin Cam or the Cosworth BDA mainly because the heavier units promote understeer.

Westfield's starter kit — Chris Smith says it needs 125-150 hours to assemble — provides the basic spaceframe, spare wheel carriers, adjustable wishbones, trailing arms, Panhard rod, stressed aluminium chassis sheeting, fixings, and glass-fibre bodywork in black,

You can have more fun in a Westfield SEI at 60mph than in a hot hatchback at 100mph. The first surprise is the amount of footroom — unlike the old Lotus 7. The Hugh Chamberlain engine is good for 110bhp with its twin 40DCOE Weber carburettors

STAN PAPIOR

white, red, blue, green or yellow, with free modification of the axle, pedal box (from a Mk1 Escort) and Austin Allegro universal joint, which has to be bought separately.

The SEI kit gives new rear suspension components, halfshaft parts and frame-mounted final drive that work in conjunction with axle back plates and halfshafts from an Escort Mk1 or 2, or Cortina Mk2. Again, these have to be supplied separately.

The Westfield extras list includes most of the parts any other manufacturer producing 700 cars a year would consider standard equipment: a windscreen, seats, hood and sidescreens, tonneau cover, even the gear lever knob. Then there are the Spax adjustable damper spring units, rollover bar, modified Minivan petrol tank, sidewinder exhaust system, wiring loom, steering column, electrical fittings, propeller shaft, engine and

gearbox mountings, air horns — vital on such a tiny car — and a host of other components. The reason for listing such vital parts as extras is that kit-car customers often already have them.

Each part is individually-priced: complete with the Chamberlain engine as tested, the SEI can be built for a little over £4000. Sales are split almost equally between the SE and SEI, with TUV-approval in Germany, homologation in Holland where there is the rival Caterham-inspired Donkervoort, testing in France and horizons in Japan next year.

And as for relationships with Caterham — which reached crisis point when the Westfield Seven looked very much like the car which took over from the original Lotus 7 — the problems are over. Now that the Westfield has been restyled as the SE or SEI it is recognisable as a marque on its own. With the new rear suspension, the marque has come of age. ∎

SEVEN UP

Colin Chapman's primal Lotus 7 has never gone out of fashion. Several companies now build variations on the Seven theme. **Roger Bell** visited Westfield in the British midlands to drive their SEi. His nerves will never be the same. Photography by **Tim Andrew**

IF OWNERSHIP OF A BRACE of Ferraris and a Porsche 911 is a symbol of success, Chris Smith, sports car nut and manufacturer, is a fair way up the ladder of achievement. Smith is the burly English midlander behind Westfield, makers of stark tearaway cars that owe their raw appeal to the legendary Lotus Seven. The Lotus connection was once such a contentious issue with establishment rival Caterham, the only company licensed by Lotus to build the late Colin Chapman's shoebox classic, that Smith was compelled in an out-of-court settlement to reshape and rename his upstart cars to distance them from the Caterham Seven look-alikes. The ensuing SE and SEi (the "i"

signifies independent rear suspension) have more rounded lines than their predecessors, but the basic formula — lightweight spaceframe carrying minimal plastic bodywork, utilitarian cockpit, and simple Ford-based running gear — is spiritually still that of a sixties Lotus.

Both outfits have continued to flourish since the legal dispute. Caterham, now based in larger premises, caters to a more affluent clientele who must wait up to a year for delivery. Although

Caterham's basic starter kits are cheap (and very incomplete), their Super Seven HPC, swiftly made up from all-new sub-assemblies, costs over $25,000 in Britain. Not counting assembly time, little more than half as much would suffice to put a Westfield SEi like the one you see here on the road. Even less using recycled components. Either way, Chris Smith's Ferraris couldn't stay with it on twisty English back roads.

Every self-built Westfield is unique, built according to its owner's whims and pocket, so there is no such thing as a standard SEi. This one is more special than most because its elderly four cylinder pushrod Ford engine has been fettled by race tuners Chamberlain Engineering of Hertfordshire, England. It doesn't just sound like a Formula Ford racer; it goes like one, too. Capacity is up from 1.6 to 1.7 liters, and power has risen from 86 to 145 bhp on a 10.4:1 compression ratio and twin Dellorto carburetors, preferred by Chamberlain to Weber units. If that horsepower figure fails to excite, consider the car's curb weight of 1100 pounds. Now raise an eyebrow. What we're looking at here is a power to weight ratio of some 290 or so horsepower per ton compared with 204 bhp per ton for a Ferrari 328, and 220 for a Porsche 911 Turbo. And that's not the end of it. In their buyer assembly guide, Westfield makes this request: "Please consult us if you intend to install more than 200 bhp." That's because the torsional rigidity of the chassis needs increasing with additional triangulation and bonded (rather than riveted) bodywork to handle really serious power. There are a couple of hillclimb specials in Britain powered by ex-Buick 3.5 liter Rover V8s shoehorned into the frame. This combination makes the power to weight ratio of a Ferrari F40 look quite tame.

Two personal accessories are needed to drive this 1.7 Westfield without acute discomfort. One is a cushion — any small household cushion will do — to tuck under the thighs and relieve aching buttocks. The other is a set of ear muffs; better still, a helmet. In such a vulnerable car, hub-high to a truck, you feel very exposed and insignificant. The side exhaust not only brands the legs of departing passengers (girlfriends beware), but also assails your hearing apparatus with rip-roaring decibels. Were this velocipede mine, I would want the exhaust to rasp from the back through something more expansive and muffling than a glorified Coke can. It can be arranged, of course. As it is, the bark burgeons to a strident cackle that presses close to the threshold of pain at 5000 rpm and beyond, especially when the sound is echoing between walls.

Few road cars can match this Westfield's explosive pounce from the traps. It takes off with demented fervor, rear tires clawing for grip, engine screaming, gears singing. On wet roads, there's such a surfeit of power over traction that you can spin rubber in third gear, never mind in first and second. More back end grip would not go amiss, though by featherweight standards the car is hardly lacking for tread blocks. Wheel spin that's fun at 20 mph, even 40, is worrying at 60 mph in a car that flicks so readily into tail-wagging power oversteer.

Anything with a 0 to 60 mph time on the slow side of 5.5 seconds will succumb to this Westfield in the dry. Thereafter, aerodynamics that make a broken brick look streamlined, peg the SEi back to sub-supercar levels, if not to humdrum ones. I never discovered its top speed and it doesn't really matter. The gearing would allow 120 mph or more, but two miles a minute in a car of suspect aerodynamic stability is faster than I would want to travel. Besides, without side screens (optional extras) the slipstream takes your breath away at 50 mph, never mind at a hundred.

There are no doors, as such, though the side screens, pivoted on the windshield uprights, must be swung clear before you can step aboard. One good reason for not having decent cloth trim is that you have to stand on it to get in. Only then can you lower yourself into the tub, shuffling limbs down the narrow footwell, single-seater style. The unadorned cockpit is tin-can tight and poorly protected from the elements. There's a simple canvas top on the options

list, but I'd sooner hide under a poncho than cower in a closed Westfield. Better to get a little wet than claustrophobic.

There's a lofty transmission tunnel embracing your hips on one side and encroaching side screens on the other, so there's not much room for flashing elbows in the SE's unadorned cockpit. Best not to get too crossed up, especially as there's little torso support, either. Imagine two prayer mats, one flat to the floor, the other leaning against the rear bulkhead, and you have a good picture of this Westfield's grim seat. Individual tailoring by the owner could no doubt remedy this uncomfortable situation, but I had to settle for an additional loose feather cushion to bolster my thighs, all the better to work the hair-trigger controls. Response to the throttle is so sharp that you shift like a boxer jabs: fast and decisively. The disc/drum brakes are

solidly weighted (there's no servo) but marvelously reactive.

Westfields of the lowest order have puny 1100 cc Ford engines, 4-speed manual transmissions, and live coil-sprung back axles located by trailing arms and a Panhard rod. Impecunious buyers in the UK can source other vital organs from their local scrapyard: suitable donors include the Ford Escort and Cortina (defunct rear-wheel drive models long since superseded) and Austin Allegro, which was the mainstream light-middleweight of Rover (Sterling in the US) until the current Maestro replaced it. The test car's 1.7 race-prepared engine was mated to a 5-speed gearbox from a Ford of Europe Sierra (Merkur XR4Ti) and Westfield's own independent rear end. It's a classy looking arrangement with wide-based upper and lower wishbones acting on special cast hub carriers to which the bottom end of the spring/damper struts are attached. This independent suspension is Westfield's answer to Caterham's de Dion rear end, and it works rather well.

Even though your backside's within scorching distance of the rear diff, never mind tarmac beneath, the ride is not uncomfortably turbulent or crashy. Firm, yes, even harsh, but free from wallow, pitch, and roll. That's as it should be for a car that tracks and grips like a circuit racer. You can't get much closer to a street legal formula car than this Westfield; it's available with front cycle fenders if you don't want hood-length swept fenders. It makes the handling of a Fiat X1/9, even a Toyota MR2, feel ponderous and lethargic. Poor self-centering marred the feel of the test car's quick but lifeless rack and pinion steering (not enough castor, perhaps) but adjustment could no doubt rectify that. Westfield allows the resourceful customer plenty of scope for inventive home engineering.

Chris Smith started his Westfield operation in 1982. Now it's the sales leader in Britain's booming kit-car market, which tempts around 3000 buyers annually with perhaps 200 different models. With a workforce of roughly 40, Westfield produces 65 kits each month and starting April 1989, another 20 completed cars exclusively for Japan, where traditional British sportsters are in great demand. All these built-up SEi's have the same 1.6 overhead cam CVH Ford engine, 5-speed transmission, and independent rear suspension.

Type Approval regulations, from which kit-cars are exempt in the UK, prevent Westfield from selling such fully assembled cars in Britain and the U.S., but they're legal merchandise in many other markets, West Germany included. Mind you, the British rules are bent almost to the breaking point by some manufacturers with kits that require minimal wrench work to complete.

Westfield has no U.S. agent (like all small specialists, Smith is wary of product liability problems here), but kits can be supplied from a daunting a la carte menu direct from the factory near Birmingham, in the heartland of Britian's motor industry. Although tailored to take European Ford engines, Toyota and Alfa twin cams have also been pressed into Westfield service. Engine bay drawings are available to help customers install non-standard powertrains.

And if the engine of choice fits but the driver does not, Westfield has the answer to that, too, in an upcoming 2.0 liter Pinto-engined variant that's three inches longer in wheelbase, and three inches wider. Why, if this heady development continues unabated, Smith will be fitting a heater next, maybe even decent seats.

Westfield's address is 5 Gibbons Industrial Park, Dudley Road, Kingswinford, West Midlands DY6 8XF, England. Phone 0384 279650, FAX 0384 288781. **SCI**

WAY OUT WEST

The little Westfield is now available as a longer and wider machine. We let our own wide boy Caddell out to get a long story on just how and why it's changed

You could be forgiven for thinking from wandering around the various bits of the Westfield operation, in Kingswinford, West Midlands, that Chris Smith's company was a particularly hyperactive section of a well known mass producer of cars not too far away. Indeed, with some 90 kits being produced each month, Westfield production really is in the 'big' league; that translates to over 1000 cars a year, a figure to make some small-scale manufacturers green with envy.

Since we took to the road last June in a little red demonstrator, things have moved on in the West Midlands. Chris is now supplying built-up cars for Japan where it seems there is an insatiable apetite for roadsters, and the cars which make it to the Orient are fitted with type-approved CVH engines. As well as churning out a batch of these, the Westfield mix, already consisting of the live-axle SE and the independent SEi, has been broadened with the wide-bodied car, available only in SEi form at £1695 plus VAT for the main kit.

Just as Caterham had to accept a few years ago that not everyone was 'Chapman-esque' and built a long-cockpit 7, so Westfield have decided that the larger among us may wish to indulge in a little roadster-type motoring — not least Mr Smith himself.

The car's chassis has been completely revamped to give an extra three inches in both directions in cockpit area, so that the seats are able to adjust and so friends travelling together don't have to be *that* close. The chassis, and the body, have been modified without adjusting the track, the extra width being taken up in the wheelarch area. And the chassis has been designed to take the overhead-camshaft Ford Pinto engine, as stocks of the 'Kent' engine are drying up fast.

The base of the Westfield is a complex square-

The bigger Westfield has certainly lost some of its style and charm in its transition from a tiny sports car to just a 'very small' one. The new Pinto engine (*above*) fits easily in the engine bay and is well placed for handling. There is much more room inside the new car for people of even slightly larger than average proportions (*left*). The twin-wishbone suspension (*far left*) could be from a formula racer tube chassis which is properly triangulated and very substantial. On the larger car, double-wishbone suspension is used all round and, with bodywork off, the rolling chassis looks for all the world like a racing car. All welding is excellent and the design is as good as you would expect for a company whose owner is an accomplished Championship-winning race driver.

There is no doubt that some of the elegance of the smaller car is lost in its transition from minimalist roadster to larger beast and it really does take a while to get used to its bloated SE looks. As for accommodation, well it really is much roomier than its snug stablemates, even though for this tester what was already on offer was a nice glove fit anyway.

The seats now adjust quite a way and there is plenty of elbow room where before there was just passenger on one side and outside world on the other. On both Westfield's demonstrators, care had been taken to make the cars' look as good as on the outside while keeping the interiors stark and bare. That would be wise when building up a car yourself as a vehicle like this will always get wet, and expensive trim will deteriorate very rapidly.

Before trying out the new Pinto car, we had a brief sortie in the machine we evaluated last year. Since that time, its Webered 1600cc Kent engine had been enlarged to 1700cc and fettled by Chamberlain who had squeezed some ridiculously high output from its pushrod

innards. Little else had changed, though, and it was still difficult to fasten the sidescreens and they didn't look that well finished once in place, anyway. And they really need to be in place when driving as the turbulence does extract most breathing material from the cockpit once the speed rises up much beyond 40mph.

With something around 150bhp to propel not much more than half a ton along, performance is shattering and the car's five-speed Sierra 'box selects ratios rapidly, if not quite as crisply as the older four-speed ones.

The car's steering is still lacking in feedback but it is as quick as you could ever want and probably too much so. It is fine when you are nipping and scything through back roads and

gently clenching fingers of either hand to effect changes in direction, but when you are hacking down a fast and straight road at a decent lick, the wheel needs constant attention as side draughts and vortices from other vehicles shake the plot around.

Back at base, it was time to try the new car, and it really does feel, as well as look, different. An open cockpit is always going to be airy, but in the larger car there really is room to manoeuvre.

Just as with the car we tried last year, the latest Pinto machine has an engine untouched by human tuner's hand other than being given a couple of gasping Dellorto 45mm carburettors to feed it. Indeed, sidedraught carburettors are not a luxury on the car but a necessity, there

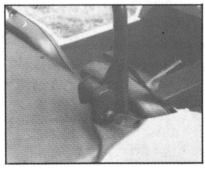

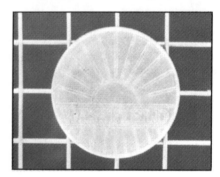

The car's inertia-reel seat belts are mounted on the roll bar which means they can be ideally placed for comfort (*top left*). The worst aspect of the car's finish is the very visible underside of the car's wings, especially the cross-bracing strut (*centre right*). There can be few more exhilarating experiences than a low-slung sports car with cutaway door apertures, fine handling and plenty of power on an open road on a sunny day. Westfield can supply most of that; you have to supply the route and the weather obviously being a distinct lack of room for a downdraught or two in the Westfield's engine bay . . . .

However, a standard, albeit deep breathing, 2-litre engine is again plenty strong enough for such a little machine, and in this particular installation there is certainly less vibration than with the Kent and much better pull from low revs. A gearbox which didn't have a proper lock on reverse and its lever tucked under the dashboard (the first a problem with a particular gearbox and the other a problem which has already been rectified) made progress a little awkward, but the urge of the motor more than made up time lost on careful gearshifting.

Probably because of the three-inch longer wheelbase, but much more probably because it was fitted with quite chunky 205/60 x 13 Avon Turbospeed tyres, there was more weight to the tiller of the longer and wider car than its more compact sister. This certainly made it feel less nervous, but then again its lack of stability on straight roads at speed still made it tiresome.

On the back roads, it proved to be nimble with no understeer just neutrality which then twitched into the back stepping sideways. The steering is naturally more than quick enough to dial in a little counter steering, but you are left feeling that a degree of understeer would be easier to live with for pushing on really quickly, giving you a point to work from progressively rather than finding out all of a sudden that the slip angle at the rear has decided to take a quantum leap in its angularity.

The ride upsets the handling when the going gets bumpy and the car skips from ridge to ridge as the occupants get bobbled around inside. However, we have experienced worse and you never buy a car like this expecting a cosseted boulevard ride. The car also suffers from a lack of ground clearance, not so much when going off road to scenic photographic locations, but on those aforementioned bumps and ridges where twice it ran out of gap 'twixt itself and the road.

The new longer and wider Westfield certainly makes a great deal of sense if you simply cannot fit in the original-sized car and it is nice having that extra room even if you are small enough not to need it. The point is that anything more than the minimum in a car of this type just gets in the way when you are using it for what it does best, and that is having huge amounts of fun on the twistiest of roads.

It was only a little while ago that Westfield announced their new model and already a third of all orders is for the new one and they expect that it will become more and more popular.

Putting together a Westfield isn't a case of bolting on the wheels and connecting up the battery but with so many parts either made or able to be supplied by Westfield, there is less heartache than with most. Westfield will supply you with a list of what will be needed in the build and probably be able to supply most bits other than the engine. From a base price of £1695, you will not be far off having enough to complete a car after a couple of trips to breakers' yards, and you should be able to get a car running for around £2500.

However, there is always a difference between a 'runner' and a decent car to live with and you can budget on £4500 plus engine and wheels and tyres to construct a machine using Westfield-sourced parts wherever possible. The point is with all vehicles like this is that you not only get what you pay for but that you can pay for it when you are able. At the end of the day in this case, though, the Westfield bits you know will be well made and more than up to the job — just like the whole car, in fact. ∎

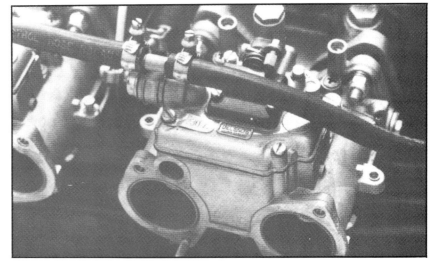

The dashboard looks a little confused (indeed, this car is a prototype) but all the switches are very close to hand (*top*). The big Dellortos are all that make this particular Pinto non standard, but all engines need sidedraught carburettors due to space restrictions (*above*). The engine itself (*left*) even mildly modded has plenty of performance from its 2 litres

HOW THE WEST HAS WON

How times change. What was once *the* vehicle for the hills of Scotland is no more. CCC bags a brace of Westfields — one with a Hewland 'box at the rear

Report David Finlay
Photography: Neil Stevenson

F ashions change. In the mid 1980s, if it became known that you had recently won an award for being top road sports car driver at an event in Scotland, your game was virtually up. "In addition to being a left-handed Mason who has spent some time in Afghanistan," Sherlock Holmes would have remarked without bothering to look up from his cornflakes, "this person owns and competes in a Caterham." And on the latter point at least he would almost invariably have been correct.

Since then, the nature of the beast has changed. Finding a Caterham on a Scottish race circuit, sprint course or hillclimb is a mostly fruitless task, foiled by the newly received knowledge that what you *really* want is a Westfield.

If you like a dash of irony in your motorsport stories, you might be interested to learn that this switch happened at about the time that Caterham won a certain court case, the outcome of which was that no Westfield should be allowed to appear with a model number between six and eight.

The new generation of 7SEs became just plain SEs (joined latterly by SEis), and almost in the same movement Scottish road car competitors took it into their heads that Caterhams were *passe* and Westfields were the cars to be seen in.

The simplest way to go Westfielding is to build up the kit, throw in a reasonably warm Ford crossflow and send off for the entry form. That formula has worked extremely well, but within Scotland's technical regulations it is possible to add shrewd ideas of your own. To cover the spectrum, we present for your attention four of the best cars, ranging from the simple but successful to the positively outlandish.

Adding a Hewland

Although he received some recognition for his performances in road-going Escorts a few years back, Neil Gammie was for some time one of the most under-rated drivers in Scotland. Most of the blame for this goes to his decidedly bleak FF2000 years in a Van Diemen which never benefited from the high budgets and testing mileages of its rivals.

Neil's return to prominence came in 1988 when he began racing in road car classes again with one of the original independent rear suspension Westfield SEis. He had placed an order for the kit in October 1987 without ever having seen more than an advertisement for the company, and this faith inspired his friend Mike Connon to follow suit.

Neil built up the kit with a rally-specification 1600 Ford crossflow engine featuring a Kent 244 camshaft, a Burton Stage 3 head and twin Weber 45 carburettors, but nothing so fancy as a steel bottom end. The power was taken to the Yokohama 185×60 tyres by an RS2000 gearbox, complete with Tran-X gear kit, and a Quaife limited slip differential.

There was nothing technically startling in all this, but it certainly worked. For the first half of the year, there wasn't another road sports car to match it on the Scottish hills, and although Connon moved ahead later on, eventually taking the road car award in the

hillclimb championship, Neil set times at Doune and Rumster which have never been approached.

On the race tracks, there was little to choose between the two, though it was fascinating to watch the contrasting styles of the exuberant Connon and the silky smooth Gammie.

The only major glitch came at a Fintray hillclimb, when a dodgy gear linkage baulked on the way into the first corner. There was no time to sort matters out, and most of the front end was wiped out against a banking.

Westfield, after being persuaded that all the car needed was a new front, not a complete chassis, were a "hell of a good company" according to Neil, who put in quite a few hours himself, stripping the car to its fundamentals and having it at the factory on the Tuesday morning.

It was over the winter that the real work started, the work which makes Neil's car so special. Out came the familiar transmission components and in went a Hewland transaxle, linked to the engine by a long propshaft running through the casing of the original Ford 'box, which was otherwise no longer there.

Choosing a Hewland was something Neil did only after "weighing the pros and cons. It was lighter for a start. I think the Hewland weighs about 60lb – the Ford 'box and diff together weigh more than 100lb. Plus the weight would be better distributed. Plus I would be able to change the gears."

This last operation was made simpler by cutting away part of the rear bodywork and refitting it in the form of a detachable panel. Remove the panel and you find yourself staring at the endplate of the transaxle, which gives you as good access to ratio-swapping as you are going to get without actually removing the 'box from the car.

As it happens, it is all a bit academic, as Neil uses only one set of cogs for all his competition. This was by no means the original plan, since he had intended to use the car for hillclimbs, Scottish circuit racing and the 750MC Kit Car Challenge.

Of these three activities, only the middle one permits the use of the Hewland 'box. That restricts Neil's competition to races at Ingliston and Knockhill, where roughly similar gears are required. The only possible difference would be a slightly higher top for Knockhill, where the engine reaches its maximum of 7200rpm at the end of each straight.

Neil's choice of gears makes for fascinating sound effects. First gear is enormously high by road car standards, being good for 55mph. Maximum speeds in the intermediate gears are reckoned to be 70 and 85mph, and the car runs out of steam at about 105mph in top. The result is a tiny drop in revs between gears, which makes life interesting inside the cockpit; as you are exiting a hairpin in first, your left hand had better be ready for action, as the next three gearchanges seem to come in about as many seconds.

That high first is not too much of a problem, partly because of the car's lack of weight. There was a slight hiccup in Neil's second race of the year, when he switched

over to Kent's racier 254 cam and bogged down on the start line. Greater care means this no longer happens, and the new cam has earned its supper by allowing the car to lap Knockhill two seconds quicker than before.

Two final points for Westfield watchers. Fitting the Hewland left no room for the middle section of the 6-gallon fuel tank. This has now become two 2-gallon tanks, one on each side of the luggage compartment and joined by a T-piece.

The other point is that, although there is only one 'box, there appear to be two gearlevers. The real one sits against the driver's left leg, but what is that object sticking out of the transmission tunnel?

That is the brake bias lever, designed to prevent the front wheels locking up too soon.

Add a Hewland 'box and there's no space for the 6-gallon tank

HOW THE WEST HAS WON

Mike Connon's solution to this was to fit harder front pads, but Neil reckoned this sounded too simple. Connon turned out to be right and Neil now has the harder pads too. Which makes the lever almost superfluous.

Still, it keeps the punters guessing.

Adding another seat

With degree exams coming up in early summer, former FF2000 racer Stuart Gray always knew that 1989 was going to be a half-and-half season. So his Reynard went on the market and, no doubt with some effort, he restrained himself from buying a replacement single-seater.

All the same, a scheme was drawn up whereby Stuart would "keep the money from the sale of the Reynard and put it towards whatever I wanted to do this year. Once my debts had been cleared and the bank manager was happy, I had just enough left over to buy a Westfield."

The Westfield in question was not a new kit but the already proven SE that Mike Connon had built and run in 1988: "You always go for the car that won the last race. That's what Mike did at Ingliston in October, and he set a new record. His was obviously the car to beat, so I went and bought it."

Engine-wise, there was practically no difference between Stuart's new car and that of Neil Gammie, though the ex-Connon machine was fitted with lighter flat-top pistons which allowed it to zip up to maximum revs very quickly. The specification has remained much the same this year, though since Stuart heard about Neil's cam change he has started pricing a Kent 254 for himself....

The rest of the car has been completely rebuilt. It was taken down to the bare chassis shortly after Stuart bought it, then pieced together lovingly by Stuart and helpers Johnny Beattie and Robert Johnston. Stuart is eager to point out that he was the least involved of the three.

"The car was being worked on two, three or four nights a week, with me helping for maybe half a night," said Stuart. "Johnny and Robert did the rest themselves while I was studying. It all worked very well – the car was ready well before the first race."

It was not, however, Stuart who did the driving in the first race, it was his brother Angus. Angus took over the reins during Stuart's exam-induced sabbatical while his own car was being built up. This is a reverse of the situation a couple of seasons ago when Stuart raced Angus's Caterham – "Angus said he was nervous watching me drive his car, and I had the same anxiety this year."

By now, a number of changes had been made to the car since its Connon days, notably a switch from restrained red to bright yellow: "Mike was amazed and almost horrified to see what we had done, adding extra weight with the paint, extra instruments, interior trim. It's now a fully fledged road car as well as an out-and-out racer."

Further, it is a useful demonstrator. Stuart regularly uses the Westfield to frighten customers of the Knockhill Racing School, where he now works. For these exercises he turns the dash-mounted rev-limiter to 6500rpm – still enough to give an impression of speed, but not so much as to compromise reliability.

For all that, Stuart has applied racing knowledge to the car too. Softer pads mean that the brakes work immediately, rather than waking up halfway round the first lap. He has also fitted a quick rack and has gone through a process of tyre experimentation which has culminated in the 185×60 Yokohamas being stretched over 7in Revolution wheels rather than the more normal 6in.

A lot of work has gone into this car since its purchase, so it seems more than a little odd that the car Stuart is most likely to race this year is the one belonging to Angus....

Adding a budget

Three years ago, there were few people contributing to Scottish motorsport to quite the same extent as Angus Gray. In his own hands, his Caterham was wildly successful in sprints – Angus became Scottish Sprint Champion in 1986 – and in those of Stuart equally so in races. It even won a couple of autotests.

By last season, things had calmed down somewhat. Stuart was well into – indeed, nearly out of – his FF2000 career, and although a rebuilt version of the Caterham was still doing well in sprints, there was nothing Angus could do if plunged into competition with a cleverly driven Westfield.

For 1989, Angus decided to switch allegiance and go for a Westfield himself. The reasons were nothing if not clear-cut.

"I wanted to stick with rear-wheel drive and with a sports car," he said. "Westfield had done a lot of development, whereas Caterham seemed to have stood still. And Caterhams are fundamentally expensive anyway.

"I sold mine for about £10,000, but if you'd unbolted all the bits, the engine, gearbox and axle would only have been worth £1500 or so. All the value was in the main body and spaceframe. It costs a fortune to build a state-of-the-art Caterham with an expensive engine, gearbox and axle. Hence the Westfield."

As you will see, the budget that would have gone into putting together a perfectly ordinary Caterham has instead been earmarked for a screamer of a Westfield. And if you're wondering why, after all that, he is doing a swap with little brother, it's because he has not been able to put nearly as much time as he would have liked into his own car.

This Westfield, an independently rear suspended SEi, is based at the family home in Edinburgh, but Angus himself is not. Job priorities resulted in a move to Manchester last September, and that meant farming out virtually the whole project to other people.

Stuart and the rest of the team have done the bulk of the preparation, with Stuart looking after the testing. The actual build-up was done by Jenvey Engineering near Birmingham and the engine, which is possibly the most impressive feature of the car, was put together by crossflow expert John Beattie.

Not that the crossflow route was the only one Angus had considered taking. There was talk in the early days of using an ex-Roger Clark 1.8-litre Cosworth unit which would have brought the car to the attention of *Astronomer's Monthly* rather than **CCC**.

"The only reason I didn't go for it was that it would have cost four grand and kept needing rebuilds," said Angus. "I put the idea to John Fyda of Agra Engineering, who said yes, it would be unbelievable, but the problem as far as he could see was that it would need a rebuild every whatever miles at a grand a time, and the chances of it going bang were pretty high."

Much the same sort of power could have been sucked out of a 2-litre 16-valve Astra unit, but getting hold of one did not look like an easy job. Which brings us back to the good old 1600cc Ford pushrod.

And what an engine it is. Everything you would want to be made of steel is made of steel, giving a potential rev limit of near 9000rpm. At the moment the limit is 8000rpm, because the hoped-for Omega pistons are not yet ready. Cam is a full-race A8 profile, and the engine breathes in through twin 48 Webers and out through a Chamberlain exhaust.

All of which adds up to a lot of oomph, though not quite as much as had been expected. Wet-sumping – to stay within road car rules – and the self-imposed narrow rev band are the main culprits.

"It seems to have lost a lot more through wet-sumping than we thought," said Angus. "We originally thought it would have 180 or 185bhp, something like that. Apparently it's about 160 – but it's a hell of a genuine 160."

One other engine worry, though it's hardly going to restrict power, is the lack of an air cleaner – "which is something I want to sort out, because the engine cost a few bob".

There is a Sierra five-speed gearbox at the back of all this, featuring a Tran-X gear kit. Tran-X is also responsible for the LSD.

But it is not just the engine that is special. The whole car bristles with serious attention to detail. Under-floor aerodynamics, Sierra Cosworth brake equipment, bottom-hinged pedals (to reduce and lower weight and to leave more room for Angus's feet), panels that are riveted *and* bonded to the chassis ... it all adds up to a package that, with Stuart driving, won first crack out of the box.

And there is nothing to suggest that the result won't 'be repeated many times in the future.

Adding a new dimension

Brian Beverly is obsessed by Avengers. His first ever car was an Avenger, and he has been competing in them ever since he took up motorsport six years ago. So you can imagine the reaction when the news broke that he was building a Westfield for the 1989 season.

A Westfield? Brian Beverley in a *Westfield*? Yes, but this one has an Avenger engine. Really? Oh, well, that's all right then.

It is not only the make of engine that distinguishes the Beverley car from the others we have mentioned. It is the size. Brian runs a 1500cc unit which puts him in the small-capacity road sports car class in Scottish hillclimbs, though not in sprints – unbelievably, the capacity split is different in the two sports.

The appeal of the class was that, although it is one of the most enjoyable and friendly in the country, nobody has ever been able to match the pace of the Ginetta drivers in the early to mid 1980s, and all the records are at least four years old. Or they were.

As Westfields became increasingly common in Scotland it was inevitable that they would attract Brian's attention. "I started thinking about them when I saw them at Ingliston a while ago. Then I had a shot in

Mike Connon's car and I thought, that's it, I'm having one," he said.

As you can imagine, 1500cc Avenger engines are not as common as they once were. The one in the Westfield came into Brian's possession by a rather tortuous route.

In 1988 Brian shared his Avenger with friend Iain Mitchell, who subsequently bought the car. The first thing Mitchell did was buy another, standard car for its shell, the race body being by now pretty crumpled. That car had a 1500 engine. Mitchell, running in the 1600cc saloon class, didn't want it, so Brian took it over for his own purposes.

Fitting an Avenger engine to a kit designed to take a Ford was not too much of a problem. All that was required was a little work on the mountings, a remote oil filter housing, to clear the steering column, and an extended-pulley system for the alternator. The only snag about that last part was that the alternators don't seem to like it much – two events is about as much as they will stand before rattling themselves to pieces.

Otherwise, the car has been very reliable, and inordinately successful. At the time of writing it had failed to win only one event, a sprint in which the main opposition was a BDG-powered Darrian. Other than that, it now holds the class record at every regularly-used hill in Scotland, and has the honour of being the fastest road car at the Kames sprint course.

All of this is a little surprising when you consider how little has been done to the car. The engine, for example, is not particularly special according to Brian.

"It's all been tuftrided and balanced by Agra Engineering. They do all my machining for me, but I do the building. It's got a big-valve head – the inlets are the biggest

you can get, but you can get bigger exhausts. Branch manifold, twin 45s ... you see those 45s? I've never had them to bits in years," said Brian.

"Incredible. It's silly when you think about it. I could probably give them to Agra and they'd give me another 20 or 30 horse. But it's not worth it till someone starts chasing me. And there's a Kent race cam, which cost me about £30."

As a couple of laps of Knockhill showed me, this package does not provide much of a kick in the back. Nor is there anything special about the transmission, which is just a standard Ford 2000E 'box – no fancy close-ratio kit – leading into an LSD.

Where the car clearly scores, apart from its useful lack of weight, is the handling, which is radically different to that of the Avenger.

"With the Avenger you had to drive at 10 or 11 tenths to get good times. With the Westfield you've got to be much more precise. Everything's got to be spot on," said Brian.

So was it a problem changing from one to the other?

"No, you just get in and think, this is great, yahoo, away we go. It just comes naturally."

Improvements? Well, the back end skips out quite a lot ("I don't know if it's me or the quick rack"), and the ratios aren't really right, and for some reason, possibly to do with the intake of air, the engine won't rev beyond 6500rpm, a good 1500 short of what an Avenger should spin to.

But the whole package is so good already that there's no point in making it any better until some heftier opposition comes along. And that is not a bad position for a car that had never seen a competition course before the end of March. ■

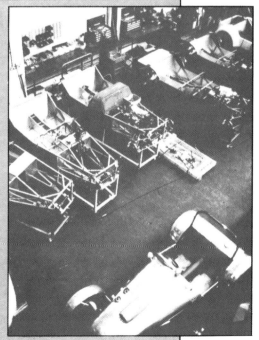

Westfield's Dudley premises are impressive. Here, the Japanese "turn-key" models are being built in view of the fabulous Lotus 6 that owner Chris Smith has just brought back from the States

MODERNS

Raw appeal from opposite ends of sportscar market

The Ferrari F40 I drove to the West Country recently for *CAR* had several things in common with the humble Westfield SE that followed it soon after. And why not? Both are uncompromising (and uncomplicated) sports cars, built to thrill and entertain. Never mind that they are separated by a couple of price-tag noughts. Both are raw driving machines with split personalities, docile one moment, ferocious the next, each with an unsettling surfeit of power over traction. Unleashed, both have the ability to generate wheelspin in third gear on greasy roads (the Ferrari in fourth, too). I'm not sure which one frightened me most in the wet.

If you think this comparison absurd, consider the common ground, starting with the need for physical dexterity to enter either. To reach the cosy embrace of the F40's winged bucket seat you have to straddle a wide, high sill of Kevlar bracing. Feeding limbs into the Westfield, poorly served by a seat that's little more than floorpan padding, is like squeezing toothpaste back into the tube.

You'll look in vain for opulent trim. Superfluous weight and cosmetic decoration are as alien to the Ferrari as they are to the Westfield. Both carry very simple instruments and switchgear, and nothing fancy in the way of equipment.

No attempt has been made to disguise the Ferrari's competition heritage. As soon as the wheels roll, its rubber rumbles and its suspension clonks. The uninsulated steel-and-Kevlar tub, carried by four pairs of very positively pivoted wishbones, seems to amplify sounds rather than suppress them. Tyre roar on concrete motorways drowns the steady snarl of the 478bhp twin-turbo quad-cam V8 behind your back.

In the test Westfield, the raucous exhaust blare of a Chamberlain - modified Ford 1700 dominates all other sounds, even wind rush in the open cockpit. Little else can be heard above its rich bark,

Ferrari F40 on the road is deafeningly loud, shatteringly quick

hysterically strident in the upper reaches. Both cars, then, are wearingly noisy, the Westfield more so than the Ferrari if you're wearing no bone dome protection – which is no bad thing to have in a car so vulnerable to attack as this lithe lightweight.

Even though fettled to give an alleged 155bhp, the SE's Dellorto-fed engine was so tractable, the car so light (under 10cwt), it would lug strongly from 1200rpm, and start in third. The Ferrari's wailing V8 is infinitely smoother and creamier than the Westfield's cackling four and even more tractable low down. It pulls cleanly from sub-idling revs but does nothing spectacular until the tacho surges beyond 3000rpm.

Like a greyhound released from its trap, the Westfield (0-60 in under 6.0seconds, if you can find the traction) is dazzlingly quick off the mark. Top speed is relatively low, though, which is perhaps just as well. I would not want to travel at much above 100mph in an open brick of suspect aerodynamic stability: 80mph feels fast enough. Compare this SE's power to weight ratio of 310bhp per ton with a Lotus Esprit Turbo's 160 per ton and a Ferrari 328's 204bhp per ton, and its explosive sprinting is easily explained. Through the

gears of its five-speed Sierra box, few cars can live with this screaming skate up to 60mph.

The F40 – crawling at 80, ambling at the Westfield's frenzied top speed of around 120mph – is something else. When the blown Ferrari's two Japanese turbos start working effectively, acceleration is truly staggering, fiercer than that of any road car I've driven before, Porsche 959 and 7.0litre Cobra included. On dry, grippy roads, the huge 335/35 rear Pirellis can handle the torque without spinning beyond first gear. You must treat the throttle with great respect in both machines.

The *grande route* Ferrari

excels as the last word in supercars on roads that you tend to avoid in the open Westfield, which takes your breath away without sidescreen protection. Conversely, the lean and agile SE is more at home than the Ferrari on tight secondaries: nothing slows a powerful monster so much as obesity when the hedges close in.

Neither car likes really bumpy roads. The SE, fitted with Westfield's own very effective independent rear suspension (in place of the usual Ford live axle) rides well and is not rattled so much by severely pocked surfaces as the F40. Still, great delicacy is needed to hold line, not least because of strangely uncommunicative steering. Were this Westfield mine, I would want to put some life – some telling wriggle and kick like that displayed by the Ferrari – into its benign helm, bereft of castor feedback. I would also want more rear rubber, less exhaust noise and a seat tailored to my torso, all of which could be arranged. Every Westfield is unique, built to satisfy the whims and pocket of its owner. No amount of wealth or influence, I'm told, will prise a bespoke F40 from Maranello.

The Ferrari's place in history was assured the day the late founder nodded his approval for the world's greatest sports car. That of the Westfield SE – whose creator, Chris Smith is a Ferrari nut and owner – will never rise above the rank of short-haul fun car. But what fun it can be, given the right roads and weather. No Ferrari, not even Nick Mason's F40, insured by *CAR* for £350,000, will give such good thrill-for-money value as a Westfield SE.

Westfield SE is no more compromised than F40. It weighs just 10cwt

IAN DAWSON

PAUL DEBOIS

Go
West

WESTFIELD SE

Testing two Westfields in two years may be two Westfields too many. Mark Hales thinks not, and welcomes the latest improvements to the marque

IT'S PROBABLY fair to say that the evolution of the Westfield SE has a great deal to do with Japan. Westfield's owner Chris Smith has sold no fewer than 250 of them to the East, and felt confident enough to open a new factory at the company's West Midlands base, now churning out Japanese spec cars at the rate of seven a week. The Japanese connection, he reckons, has doubled his turnover at a stroke. Quite why Westfield should succeed where Caterham has all but failed is something of a mystery to me, Smith attributes it to a "different marketing strategy". Suffice it to say that there are 28 Westfield dealers in Japan, who, amongst other things, relay the news that 40 percent of Westfield purchasers already own a Porsche or a Ferrari.

There's nothing like a ready market to stimulate development, and the subject of this test is a much more refined animal than the example I tested two years ago. (*Fast Lane*, June 1988), although the minimalist driving-machine-above-all concept still remains. A 1,600cc XR2 Fiesta engine replaces the previous Kent crossflow options, and is largely unmodified save for some small head and cam revisions to make Ford's lean-burn fuel efficiency concept more suitable for the attachment of a pair of snorting side-draught 40DCOE Weber carburettors. Power output is raised a touch from the Fiesta's 100 to a claimed 120bhp at 6,000rpm, but the Webers are

ROADTEST

"The Japanese will not have anything other than Webers adorning their underbonnets"

as much cosmetic as anything else. Smith is adamant that the Japanese will not have anything other than Webers adorning their underbonnets — even the outwardly similar Dellorto was rejected because it didn't have the right name.

The Webers also contribute to the driving experience in that they make nearly as much noise as the exhaust, which is considerable. The raucous gasping that emanates from the underbonnet in response to full throttle is still undeniably a joyful experience that will appeal to even the most jaded of enthusiasts.

Another vast improvement is also provided by Mr Ford, and a five-speed overdrive-top Sierra gearbox replaces the Cortina four-speeder, at the same time handily moving the gear lever further along the transmission tunnel, nearer the driver. This off-the-peg Ford hardware has the desired effect of adding a little class which was missing in previous Westfields, and it makes the car feel much more together than its predecessor. You are sitting low and tugging at the shortened Sierra lever (at elbow height of course), but the change snicks through as fast as you care to move the lever, and you wouldn't guess the origin of the transmission from the evidence. Gearing which only yields a top speed of just over 100mph closes up the ratios so you can play tunes up and down the gearbox at almost legal speeds, while monitoring the effectiveness of your composition beneath the passenger's elbow.

The joy of zipping up and down gears just for the hell of it represents a prime part of the total experience, and makes the car feel rather quicker than the test track figures reveal. The initial acceleration is limited by traction, while the upper regions are hampered by the aerodynamics of a sail. Not that you'd want to cruise at 100mph anyway – the noise and wind should be sufficient deterrent, hood up or down. Nevertheless, there aren't many cars that will comfortably slip below the seven seconds to 60mph barrier, and even fewer at the Westfield's price tag.

Without the constraining needs for road refinement, magic carpet ride quality and idiot-proof handling, it is not too difficult to make a simple sports car handle well, and the Westfield retains its race car responses, along with proven double wishbone independent suspension at both ends. Some components have been changed here in the interests of ease of service and supply; Sierra 4×4 front drive components appear at the SE1's rear – the "1" denoting independent rear suspension, as it is still possible to buy a kit ready to accept a Mk2 Escort solid rear axle. Westfield-manufactured aluminium front uprights have by now replaced the Cortina Mk4 items, and Smith reckons to have ensured a continued supply of Mk2 Escort differentials to go inside the special alloy diff-housing.

A spindly collection of fabricated tubular wishbones and skinny coil springs unites wheel and chassis, and still surprising is the ride quality that it produces, a feature you tend not to expect with

a little clubman racer concept. The SE1 takes moderate bumps well with no tendency to hop at the rear under power, although very sharp imperfections will rattle the car off its line.

Powering hard through a tightish corner, the SE will just understeer progressively, more as you push on harder, until eventually an inside wheel will start to spin, effectively cutting the power. You can unbalance the car by braking into the bend as you turn the wheel, but you have to try pretty hard – and while it may not have been a prime development objective, the handling is all but prat-proof. Light weight allows simple dampers to provide good body control, even with comparatively soft suspension.

The car's handling integrity is beyond reproach, and the response to inputs sharp without being over sensitive, but to my mind the steering still lacks a little feel. It's not a question of steering weight, more the need for greater communication from the road surface, a little kickback or wriggle at the wheel rim; sensations which help to sense impending loss of grip. At the moment it has a rather oddly remote feel, which is completely at variance with the intimate nature of the car.

Given that the Westfield and its ilk are items of automotive clothing, to be worn rather than simply used, it is pleasing to report that seats are better than they were, although why the manufacturer didn't go the whole way and make a proper bucket shape, rather than a traditional '60s squab and back, is beyond me. Last year's Westfield made you feel rather vulnerable, as if the driver was perched rather than ensconced, and although this latest example feels better to me, the sensation of being fully part of the car is still a touch lacking. In this respect, the Caterham still has the edge, at a price.

Westfield weather equipment is either a wimpy superfluity, or a pneumonia-avoidance protection, depending on your point of view. Smith tends to subscribe to the former opinion, but the hood and the sidescreens could be better without adding significantly to the cost. That, and the seats, are all that's really left to make the full transformation from occasional fun car to reasonably practical road burner.

The Westfield has never needed any excuses dynamically. It's well made and well sorted, and every model gets better. The next one apparently features pull-rod suspension at the front and is likely to be powered by either the Peugeot Mi-16 twin cam or the Ford Sierra two-litre double-overhead-cam unit, and some of my moans have been addressed. The price is going up of course – the test car will continue to be available and costs £10,850 including taxes – which given the performance is still good value for money.

WESTFIELD SE1

PRICE £10,850 inc taxes. In order to avoid type approval, the car needs about 20 hours' work to make roadworthy.

ENGINE

CYLINDERS	four, in-line
CAPACITY, cc	1,596
BORE/STROKE, mm	80 × 79.5
CAMSHAFT	sohc, two valves per cylinder
COMPRESSION RATIO	9.5:1
FUEL SYSTEM	twin Weber 40DCOE side-draught twin-choke carburettors
MAXIMUM POWER, bhp/rpm	120/6,000
MAX TORQUE, lb ft/rpm	101/4,000

TRANSMISSION

TYPE	five-speed synchromesh, rear wheel drive
INTERNAL RATIOS AND MPH/1,000rpm	
Fifth	0.82:1
Fourth	1.0:1
Third	1.37:1
Second	1.97:1
First	3.65:1
FINAL DRIVE	3.9:1

CHASSIS

SUSPENSION	
Front	upper and lower wishbones, coil springs anti-roll bar
Rear	independent, upper and lower wishbones, coil springs
STEERING	rack and pinion
BRAKES	
front/rear	disc/disc
WHEELS	6×14in aluminium alloy
TYRES	185/60 HR14 Avon Turbospeed

DIMENSIONS

LENGTH, in	WIDTH, in	HEIGHT, in	WHEELBASE, in
139.4	61.4	43.3	91.9

TRACK front/rear, in	FUEL TANK, gall	KERB WEIGHT, cwt
52.1/52.0	00.0	11.2

PERFORMANCE

MAXIMUM SPEED, mph 102.9

ACCELERATION THROUGH GEARS, sec

0-30	0-40	0-50	0-60
2.5	3.7	5.0	6.9

0-70	0-80	0-90	0-100
8.8	11.8	16.3	24.8

ACCELERATION IN FOURTH, sec

30-50	40-60	50-70	60-80	70-90
5.5	5.5	6.8	6.5	7.2

ACCELERATION IN FIFTH, sec

30-50	40-60	50-70	60-80	70-90
7.9	8.1	8.0	10.7	12.8

MAKER: Westfield Sports Cars Ltd, 5 Gibbons Park, Dudley Road, Kingswinford, West Midlands DY6 8XF. Tel: 0384 279650

POWER TO WEIGHT

WESTFIELD S EIGHT

0-100mph in 8.5sec from something you could buy for £10,000? Sounds like a job for Mark Hales

LAST MONTH'S cover suggested two ways to blow off a Ferrari. I would like to suggest a third, with the added condition that the means must be fully road legal, usable on a regular basis . . . and cost less than £10,000. It should also be reasonably viceless – as much as anything capable of that sort of performance is likely to be.

I recently spent a few days with the prototype version of Westfield's Rover V8 powered Seven – a simple amalgam of large engine and small chassis, which is the oldest recipe of all for startling performance. Now, I'm not sure why, but the very suggestion of eight cylinders in something the size of a Westfield brought gasps of horror from friends and colleagues, most of whom would not have batted an eyelid at the thought of a four-cylinder, belt-driven Ford pushing out similar amounts of power at half as many rpm again. Why use an expensive, frenetic 16-valve small displacement engine when you can use a large, cheap and lazy one to achieve a similar result?

The Rover Vitesse engine and five-speed manual gearbox drops in the now familiar Westfield chassis with remarkably little trouble and, from the outside, the only giveaways to an increase in the cylinder department are an exhaust on each side and a lump in the bonnet. The all-aluminium engine is a compact unit. It's not much

F40 and Westfield share similar performance and minimal comforts, but cheaper car has leather trim, too . .

longer than a two-litre four, and it looks completely at home under the Westfield's minimal fibreglass lid. The latter will sport either the aforementioned discreet bump, or a hole, depending on the induction system selected by the customer. The rest of the chassis differs little from the basic XR2-powered versions. The prototype featured Westfield's regular twin wishbone per side independent rear suspension, straddling the specially cast housing for the Escort Mk2 differential with its Salisbury limited slip. Production cars will utilise the unbreakable Sierra/Granada diff, a solution favoured by both TVR for the S and by Caterham for its Seven. Front suspension on the V8 is standard twin wishbone, with slightly stiffer coil springs to prop up the extra weight, while the brakes, solid discs both front and rear, have needed no attention to cope with the extra urge.

The Rover engine now comes in either 3.5 or 3.9-litre guise, and the test car featured the larger unit with a few mild tweaks performed by Rover specialist J E Motors in Coventry. The reciprocating bits had been balanced and carefully assembled, compression ratio raised to around 9.75:1, and a mild solid-lifter cam operates standard-sized valves. Four Dellorto 45mm twin-choke downdraught carburettors supply polished ports with leaded four-star. The carburation appeared to be rather an overkill given the previous affirmation that the power unit was to be inexpensive as well as large, but JE assured me that much the same power output could be achieved with a simpler set-up, or even the standard electronic injection. The test car's engine develops 268bhp at 6,000rpm, and the all-up weight is a little over 1,389lb.

The results of this combination are simply shattering. I can think of no other production car within four, maybe 10, times the Westfield's price which can sprint in similar fashion. From a standing start, 30mph came up in just 1.9sec, the sort of time normally reserved for super-tractive Porsches or four-wheel-drive machinery – and then on to the magic 100mph took a staggeringly brief 8.5sec in total, 60mph a trifling 4.0. And although it was undeniably exciting and not a little raucous, it was achieved with a minimum of drama. Normally such lightweights sit for a reflective moment while the rear tyres catch fire before they get going, and the absence of this is additional proof of the big engine's worth. Because it develops its power from low down, you don't need to take on a load of wheelspin to match the engine's working range to the first gear ratio. You gently take your foot from the clutch with 1,000rpm showing on the rev-counter, and simultaneously plant the right foot.

The in-gear acceleration figures were predictably, something else again. In fourth, 60-80mph needed 2.5sec, in fifth 3.7. We never recorded any in-gear times for the Ferrari F40, but a look at the standing start figures in the April '89 issue reveals zero to 60 in 3.9sec and 100 in 7.8. The test Westfield has accelerative performance which is genuinely in the Ferrari F40 class. It won't reach 200mph of course, although

"The Westfield has accelerative performance which is genuinely in the F40 class"

it will better 130mph. That's a good deal faster than you'd want to cruise, given the accompanying noise level and draughts.

The level of performance is perhaps only as much as you'd expect, given 1,389lb and 268bhp, but more important is the sheer ease with which it is achieved. The engine, even in mildly tuned form, is utterly docile and will pull from 1,000rpm in fifth. In fact, you lose very little acceleration by so doing, and you can potter round town all day in any of the higher gears. You can even start from rest in fourth without much slip if you want. Neither is there any sudden rush of motivation as the revs rise. There's always power, at any rpm, and the driver has total control over the force pressing in the back by simply moving the right foot. Down for the force, lift to stop. It's quite intoxicating and, I believe, given a modicum of common sense, safer than a small screamer which peaks at an awkward

moment and gives the suspension something sudden to think about.

The instant grunt also gives the chassis a nice balance, I always felt that the lower powered versions would tend to push on wide if you accelerated through a corner, but with the addition of so much lazy horsepower you can keep progress neutral without needing to be a hooligan and bang the tail wide. It *will* do that if you want of course, but it's easy enough to catch provided you don't allow it to go too far. Understeer does not feature in this car's vocabulary, but it's not wild. Neither do you need to commit the car to a corner in any particular way, you can just brake smoothly and early and power through text-book style with a minimum of work at the wheel. Recommended wheels are 7 x 15in aluminium split rims shod with grippy 205/50 Goodyear NCT rubber.

The Westfield's steering has gained a little weight with the heavier engine, which is welcome, but it could still do with a little more feel. It lacks that delightful alive and springy feeling of some of its ilk.

So, given that it's not the irresponsible monster that most people thought, can all this performance really be available for less than £10,000? The answer is a qualified yes, given that you'd have to do some of the work on the engine on the cheap, or forego some creature comforts, plus you'd need to spend the odd weekend wielding a spanner. The possibilities are many and varied, but using brand new bits everywhere, it splits like this. Westfield will not sell the chassis other than as a fully-assembled item with no used parts whatever, and with exhausts, aluminium wheels and tyres, hood, trim and instruments, the total is £7,200 plus VAT. They reason that, given the available performance, they would rather ensure that everything is properly assembled. The customer can, however, supply his own wheels and tyres, trim and instruments, and forego the weather equipment in which case the bill drops to £4,750. The engine in the test car totalled £6,000, but a fully rebuilt, intermediate spec V8 from J E Motors, based on a reasonable donor engine (usually around £500) and breathing through a simple pair of SU carburettors, would produce around 220bhp and cost in the order of £3,000. Alternatively (and this would be my preferred option), you could opt for a brand new 190bhp 3.9-litre which, complete with new five-speed gearbox, clutch, starter, gearlever and all ancillaries like alternator and water pump, is available from J E for £3,900. The test car would cost about £14,000 (plus the poll tax support) to duplicate, including somebody's wages to fit the engine.

So, your £10,000 might enable you to see off most ordinary Ferraris, but if you want to deal with the odd upstart F40, you will need to spend that little extra.

WESTFIELD S EIGHT

ENGINE

CYLINDERS:	eight in a vee, all alloy, front longitudinally-mounted
CAPACITY, cc:	3,900
BORE/STROKE, mm:	94/71.1
VALVE GEAR:	cams in block halfrace with solid lifters and adjustable push rods, two valves per cylinder
COMPRESSION RATIO:	9.75:1
FUEL/IGNITION SYSTEM:	four downdraught 45DRLA Dellortos
FUEL:	four star leaded only
PEAK POWER, bhp/rpm:	274/6,000
PEAK TORQUE, lb ft/rpm:	285/4,500
POWER/WEIGHT RATIO, bhp/ton:	441.9

TRANSMISSION

TYPE:	five-speed all synchromesh Rover SD1 gearbox driving the rear wheels through a limited-slip differential

INTERNAL RATIOS AND mph/1,000rpm

fifth	0.792:1/23.7
fourth	1:1/18.8
third	1.396:1/13.4
second	2.087:1/8.9
first	3.321:1/5.7
final drive	3.54:1

CHASSIS

SUSPENSION front:	independent via unequal length wishbones, coil springs and telescopic dampers
rear:	independent via unequal length wishbones, coil springs and telescopic dampers
STEERING:	rack and pinion manual
BRAKES, front/rear:	solid disc/solid disc no assistance
WHEELS:	7 x 15 120mm inset aluminium alloy rims
TYRES front:	195/50/15 Goodyear NCT Eagles
rear:	205/50/15 Goodyear NCT Eagles

DIMENSIONS (inches)

LENGTH	WIDTH	HEIGHT	WHEELBASE
139.4	61.4	43.4	93.0

TRACK, front/rear	FUEL TANK, gal	KERB WEIGHT, lb
51.6/52.4	6.0	1,389

PERFORMANCE (mph)

MAXIMUM SPEED, mph: 130

ACCELERATION THROUGH THE GEARS, mph/sec

0-30	0-40	0-50	0-60	0-70
1.9	2.7	3.3	4.0	5.0
0-80	**0-90**	**0-100**	**0-110**	**0-120**
6.0	7.2	8.7	10.4	13.3

ACCELERATION IN FOURTH/FIFTH, mph/sec

30-50	40-60	50-70	60-80
3.0/ –	2.7/3.8	2.4/3.7	2.4/3.8
70-90	**80-100**	**90-110**	**100-120**
2.6/3.8	2.7/4.0	3.2/4.4	– /5.4

PRICE AS TESTED INC TAXES Around £16,500 (see text)

IMPORTER Westfield Sports Cars, 5 Gibbons Industrial Park, Dudley Road, Kingswinford, West Midlands, DY6 8XF. Tel: 0384 279650

7 days with The Brute

It was a week we'll never forget, a week spent getting to grips with a 270bhp Westfield V8 that goes like a Ferrari F40

Day 1, 10am, Peterborough

Robert Davies takes delivery

Phone call from reception — the Westfield's arrived. Ah, the SEiGHT. With its 270bhp V8, I manage to tear myself away from writing captions and rush out to pick up the keys. Two hundred and seventy bhp, eh? Four hundred and forty one bhp per ton, someone said. Exactly the same as a Ferrari F40. Mmm. . . maybe I could spare time for a quick spin round the block. Check it's not raining first — don't want *that* sort of spin.

And here is The Brute, with its keeper. He looks calm enough. No wonder; he's towed it here on a trailer.

'It's all yours. Nothing special you need to know.' Keeper turns to leave, stops on an afterthought. 'Oh, it's been spitting back through the carbs. Probably nothing. But we put in a fire extinguisher just in case. Have fun.'

Umm. . . perhaps I should let someone else try it first. Those captions are urgent after all.

What the hell. Slide inside, sort out feet on narrow pedals, ignore rows of blank switches, take a deep breath, fire up the beast and burble out of car park.

Third gear, 3000rpm. Grit teeth. Floor throttle. BROARRRR! Someone thumps me in the back with lump of concrete, head snaps back, road blurs. WHOOOSHHH! Cockpit fills with mist. What the hell's going on? The bloody fire extinguisher's rolled loose and gone off in my face.

Back off throttle, extinguisher rolls

The Brute

back, whooshing stops. But — RATATATATAT — deafening artillery barrage breaks out behind my ears, exhausts backfiring frantically on the overrun. Carburettors let loose a couple of ominous belches too.

All drowned out by my pulse beating a heavy metal rhythm. This car is serious. And possibly possessed. Two hundred and seventy bhp? I can handle it, no problem. But not just now. I've got some captions to write. Calderwood can take it home.

Day 1, 5.30pm
Dave Calderwood takes The Brute home to meet the family

First job is to squeeze my 6ft 2in, 13-stone frame into the roller-skate, with the hood up (since it's drizzling). Left leg in first, push down into the footwell as far as it can go; bum next, then fold the right leg as tight as possible to hoike it in, taking care not to wipe the steering wheel with a wet shoe.

There's a prob: my size 11 shoes overlap the pedals. Touching the brakes also blips the throttle. So, it's off with the shoes, an exercise conducted in situ and not easy. I'll drive home in socks.

The Rover V8 engine, tuned by JE Motors, sounds menacing even at tickover, snarling at the merest hint of throttle. Rover's five-speed gearbox, with a short, stubby lever, is predictably difficult to shift, especially into reverse. First task is to brim the tank, testing my patience — and that of the queue behind me — because the filler neck regurgitates if fed at more than a trickle.

Eventually, we're away down the A1 and as soon as a gap appears I floor the throttle. The engine spits back and a cloud of white petrol vapour fills the car — thank God I don't smoke. Within what seems like no time at all we're doing . . . a very high speed that I'd rather not put in print. We got there courtesy of a bonnet full of what sounds like an angry team of Gas Board roadwork navvies, jackhammering and pneumatic drilling away as though on triple time AND a beat-the-penalty-clause bonus.

The noise is extraordinary, the power pulsing through the little car is extraordinary, the scenery flashing past so close is extraordinary . . . this is Sensurround motoring and I've covered the 55 miles home to Knebworth in a ridiculous time, fuel gauge showing half-empty. Why couldn't I slow down? I don't know, I just couldn't.

> ## 'Now it's generating the odd explosion through the sidewinder exhausts. People are staring'

Day 2, 8am
Calderwood takes The Brute to the test track

I'm due to meet road test editor Barker at Millbrook, the test circuit near Bedford where we measure

● What's a nice fire extinguisher like you doing in a car like this?

● Long division: a 6ft tall driver into a 3ft high car does not go (easily)

performance. My usual route through Herts and Beds follows tiny country lanes where earth banks and hedges sit either side of a narrow carriageway. This doesn't appeal in a car with a roof height lower than your dangly bits so I opt for a more open route via Hitchin.

Mistake; the early morning traffic is dog slow. The Westfield doesn't like this and the exhaust sounds even louder when surrounded by traffic. And then there's the pops and bangs on the overrun, spitting back through the Dellorto carbs (with twin foam air filters poking out of the bonnet) and generating the odd huge explosion through the sidewinder exhausts. People are staring.

At last, the occasional gap starts to appear and a game of overtaking begins. There's no need to change down — leave the Westfield in third or fourth and use the motor's massive amounts of instantly available torque to blast past. I hop up the line in a series of abrupt manoeuvres: pop out for a look-see, gas it hard from 40 to 80mph in an instant, leaving the ground behind trembling (or so it seems), off the gas and use the tremendous engine braking to slot in: there's no need to touch the excellent brakes. Schoolkids leer at me from the back window of a coach, cheer as I pull out to overtake, then go wide-eyed as the noise hits them. As I pull back in ahead, I can only imagine what effect the thunderflash backfires are having.

At Millbrook I hand over the car to Barker with some relief.

Day 2, 10am, Millbrook Proving Ground
John Barker goes for the times of his life

'I've only got one crash helmet,' says Calderwood apologetically but I'm sure what he means is 'I only brought one helmet so that I don't have to be in the car for the maximum speed run.' There's

● No smoke without fire . . . Westfield burns 0-60 dash in just 4.4 seconds

● An awful lot of engine and not very much car — the Westfield's 3.9-litre V8

● A bit of a brute. Gearchange is a little on the heavy side, like stirring concrete

an easy way to tell if I'm right: 'That's OK; I've brought one, too,' I say, cheerfully. Calderwood comes clean and says he'd rather not be in The Brute at full tilt. As he's driven it here, this worries me slightly. Westfield's Chris Smith reckons it'll top 145mph.

With head encased by Kevlar and expanded polystyrene, the sound of wind roaring around the hood and the bellow of the V8 are muted. And although the chassis squirms dramatically over the bowl's notorious bump, the car feels otherwise quite stable. I reckon on 135mph, tops. Maybe not; on one lap, a Porsche 944 Turbo gets in the way.

The stopwatch shows that the steel-framed, glassfibre-bodied SEiGHT has just lapped at 144mph. Gulp. A cool 150mph on the flat seems quite feasible. Stunning though this is, it's the acceleration times that make the most interesting reading.

If you want proof that 270bhp is about 100bhp more than a lightweight, rear-

● Guilty of disturbing the peace: Westfield frightens horses too

drive car like the Westfield can usefully employ, consider this; even starting in second gear, the SEiGHT hits 60mph from rest in 4.4 seconds, and you still have to be careful not to induce rampant wheelspin.

In terms of pure overtaking ability, the SEiGHT trades punches with the world's best supercars. From 40-80mph takes 3.7 seconds. Think about it. A Ferrari F40, the quickest of them all, does it in 3.2. The F40 dispatches the quarter mile in 12.1 seconds, the

Westfield 12.7. Which is all well and good if the road is smooth, clear and dry, but over the next two days the roads were far from that. It p*ssed it down.

Day 3, 8am, Leighton Buzzard

Barker drives to work. In the rain

The short wipers are flicking across the screen at a demented pace, water is creeping in under the door to soak my elbow and there's a vibration that gets quite nasty above 60mph. Neither of us is very happy today. Yesterday's performance testing rattled something loose in the transmission and until we get it up on a ramp to see if it's serious, I'm avoiding using full throttle.

Not that I could if I wanted to. The chassis is generally well sorted but gets thrown by big bumps, and some of my favourite road's bumpier sections are making half throttle seem far too much, the grip of the fat Goodyears breaking in fourth gear at times, demanding razor sharp corrections.

Later in the day, the vibration is traced to loose propshaft bolts; one is missing, two are loose and the fourth is hanging bravely in there. Replacements will meet deputy editor Tomalin at Bruntingthorpe tomorrow. For now, those that remain are tightened and the sodden B660 back to Leighton Buzzard beckons once more.

Day 4, 9am, Peterborough

Barker has survived a second rain-sodden journey to work

I arrive soaked once more but happy. The SEiGHT's chassis is far from perfect but it is predictable: if the engine sounds like it's working, the car will go sideways. If this occurs in a bumpy corner it will go very sideways. You need to treat it as you would a powerful motorbike in the wet; go gingerly through the corners and step on it down the straights. Yes, 270bhp is too much but you never tire of trying to use it.

Day 4, 11.30am

Peter Tomalin takes The Brute to have its picture taken

Once you're wedged in, strapped in and locked in, there's no escape. The Brute has you in its grip. The key in your dripping palm is like the damp, dog-eared ticket to the scariest fairground

The Brute

ride of them all. You've gone past the barrier, your friends are watching your eyes and there's no turning back.

Now, turn that key. You know what to expect but it's still a shock. A metallic attack, a fusillade from two sawn-off shotguns masquerading as exhausts. You don't just *hear* this sort of noise — you *feel* it, deep in your bones.

And as you trickle along with the traffic, hardly daring to breathe on the throttle, you're being drawn inexorably to that first open straight, the first heartstopping plunge of the big dipper, the moment you simply have to unleash The Brute.

'Take it to Bruntingthorpe,' they tell

● *It's a tight squeeze in there. Editor Calderwood had to take his shoes off*

● *Westfield looks a real beastie — from almost any angle . . .*

me. 'Get some pictures. Standing starts, sideways round corners, that sort of thing. If it's wet you'll have no trouble getting it sideways . . .' I can still hear their slightly malevolent chuckles as I skirt the car park puddles and approach the Westfield, squatting sullenly under a leaden sky. The rain has stopped, but the blacktop is glistening . . .

The devil made me do it. Creeping out of a T-junction, no other cars around and with just a hint of steering lock, I slot second and pull the trigger. Bad move. The Brute snaps, snarls and flicks out its tail. A dab of opposite lock reins it in, but I've learned the first lesson.

Bruntingthorpe. Dry track. Playtime! I thought it would be easy, serving up lurid oversteering slides to order. It isn't. First, the Westfield's wide, wide rear boots take some unsticking. By the time they really let go in the dry you're fairly flying, the g-forces tugging you out of shape. Second, it takes real delicacy to steer it accurately on the hair-trigger throttle, releasing just enough horses to hold the slide. It takes practice. And that takes a deserted test track.

Standing starts next. On Barker's advice I select second, gun the engine to 4000rpm and sidestep the clutch. Finally free, The Brute hurtles towards the

horizon, tyres wailing, rear end jinking this way and that, tiny wheel dancing a jig in my hands as I fight to hold course, snatching third and hearing the tyres wail again . . .

Who's next?

Day 5

Calderwood has second thoughts

The initial shock of the Westfield has worn off, so now's the time for a more considered evaluation. I hate it.

It's all very well saying you can't have too much power but in the Westfield V8's case, the very bulk of the engine dominates the car's behaviour. Take this Westfield down an undulating lane and instead of following the crests and dips faithfully, the weight of the drivetrain takes the car where it wants. Similarly, on a twisty road, instead of switching from right to left precisely and accurately, you've got to allow an extra few inches; that motor needs some persuading to change line.

Lastly, the engine isn't one of JE Motors' best. We've driven others, notably a tuned Range Rover V8, that are sweet and torquey. This one's a beast, a socially unacceptable pitbull terrier just waiting to slip its leash.

Day 6

Tomalin picks up the pieces

Remember the propshaft bolts? They weren't the only bits to break on the

SEiGHT during our short tenure, though *most* of it wasn't the car's fault. First the screen cracked on the Millbrook bowl (just rotten luck). Then the tiny straps that hold the sidescreens in place snapped (this happens to Caterhams too; it's something owners sort out themselves). Then someone who shall be nameless clipped the scoop under the front of the engine and that fell off. Then someone who shall be nameless (oh, all right, it was Barker) dented the sump (you'll have gathered by now that ground clearance is not great — it's in the python class, actually). Then the engine boiled over at Bruntingthorpe. And all this accompanied by those mighty backfires from the nearside exhaust on over-run (the mixture wasn't correctly adjusted),

> ## 'I turn the key, dab the throttle, and the Westfield sounds as if it's going to eat me'

and the clouds of petrol vapour that occasionally filled the cockpit — three different drivers got the shock of their lives when the instrument lights suddenly dropped down and dangled in the footwell, looking for all the world like the beginnings of a fire.

What the heck — if you buy a car like the Westfield (you'll pay around £16,500 for a complete top-spec car like ours, as little as £4750 plus VAT for the engine and chassis) you expect to get your hands dirty. Call it character. The Brute has that in abundance.

Day 7

PC designer Martin Mulchinock has the final fling

As I am never allowed to forget, I'm Nova Man. My four-year-old Vauxhall Nova 1.3SR may be a capable little runabout, but with only 72bhp it's almost 200bhp less exciting than the SEiGHT. Now I slot myself into another world. The outlook is like nothing I've experienced before; sitting below the tops of lorry wheels and staring up other people's exhaust pipes.

Turn the key, dab the throttle and the Westfield sounds as if it's going to eat me. First and second gears just happen, and if you're not very careful the Law is what happens next.

Conversation in the SEiGHT, when you can make yourself heard, tends to revolve around test pilots breaking the sound barrier, fighter aircraft, and other life-threatening pursuits. Decelerating

● **TURN THAT NOISE DOWN!** Hood-up, it's like sharing cockpit with Motorhead

● Flat out, Westfield will do 145mph. But it feels more like 245mph . . .

into villages The Brute snaps and crackles, and we feel like gun-slingers riding into town. 'Yeeehaaaaa!'

In the Nova every overtaking manoeuvre takes careful planning — not in The Brute. This car gives you a Red Baron mentality, its little windscreen and A35 wiper blades taking the place of WW1 goggles. I start gunning down the XR3s which make my life in the Nova hell. Such satisfaction.

As a motorcyclist, I notice some real parallels besides performance: the lack of storage space, the noise, smells and draughts, plus a need to keep a wary eye on surface imperfections. You really have to think about when to press the fire button under your right foot.

The Westfield SEiGHT — only Alton Towers offers a ride that comes close. ○

	Westfield SEiGHT	Ferrari Testarossa
ENGINE	V8, 3.9 litres, front	Flat 12, 5.0 litres, mid
POWER	270bhp at 6000rpm	390bhp at 6300rpm
TORQUE	285lb ft at 4500rpm	361lb ft at 4500rpm
BHP/LITRE	69.2	78
KERB WEIGHT	1371lb	3650lb
POWER TO WEIGHT	441bhp/ton	239bhp/ton
PERFORMANCE	(secs)	(secs)
0-30mph	2.2	2.2
0-60mph	4.4	5.3
0-100mph	9.4	11.3
0-130mph	21.5	19.9
¼ mile	12.7	13.6
4th gear 30-50	3.6	5.0
50-70	2.9	5.0
70-90	3.1	4.8
5th gear 50-70	4.4	7.3
70-90	4.8	7.7
90-110	5.0	8.2
MAX SPEED	144mph	180mph

A diesel called

Mix a lightweight roadster with a modified turbocharged diesel unit. You get a 'green' sports ca

Finished, it drives like a production car

Modified diesel engine gives 110bhp

PETER BURN

Weasel

quicker than a BMW M5. Steve Cropley reports

IT'S THE 30-70MPH ACCELERATION time which shouts loudest. The Weasel — a recently-built experimental Westfield SE sports car powered by a 'hot' turbo diesel — is faster through the gears than a BMW M5, a Ford Sapphire Cosworth 4x4 and an Audi S2. It gives the Lancia Delta Integrale 4x4 a very good run for its money too.

Its top gear 50-70mph times are even more remarkable. There, the Westfield diesel beats all of the cars previously named plus the Aston Martin Virage, the BMW M3 Evolution, the Lotus Elan SE and the Porsche 928 S4, and is only just shaded by the manual BMW 850i.

But here's the punch-line: this experimental oil-burner from the Black Country accelerates just as quickly as these high-bred icons of high performance — but it will also travel at least two and a half times as far as they do on a gallon of fuel. An average fuel consumption for the Westfield Weasel, still in its very first flush of development, is 60mpg.

The question is, who'd want to build a turbo diesel sports car? According to the rule book, diesel engines are not supposed to power really fast cars. Their job is to propel sensible, flexible models with miserly fuel consumption and clean exhausts: cars for people whose priorities are a million miles away from true high performance.

The trouble is, turbo development engineer Richard Wilsher has not read the rules. He believes properly developed turbo diesels are the high-efficiency, low consumption engines tomorrow's performance cars will need — and to prove it he's bolted one of his own modified Ford Sierra diesels into a Westfield SE chassis and come up with a car which can knock spots off most Porsches for acceleration — yet can pull economy figures to equal a Citroen AX diesel out of the hat as well.

"For years, I've believed in the efficiency of diesels, and particular of turbo diesels," says Wilsher, whose background includes a stint as a grand prix engineer during the late '70s and years spent designing petrol turbo systems both for production cars and for the aftermarket. These days he operates his own engineering development business, Sword Automotive, in Mark, Somerset. "As time goes on, fuel will get much more expensive," he predicts. "The kind of economy diesels can deliver will become more and more important. I aim to show that fuel efficient diesels cars can be as fast as anyone could want."

At first, Wilsher had no thought about cars for his experiment, only the engine. He acquired a 1.8-litre Ford turbo diesel a couple of years ago and set about improving its middle to top end power and torque, without destroying its economy or low-end flexibility. The aim was to increase the standard engine's 75bhp at 4500rpm to around 120bhp at more or less the same crank speed, with a commensurate increase in torque. The modifications included changes to the engine's combustion chamber shapes to improve swirl (he refuses to be more specific), a bigger Garrett turbocharger than the standard T2, redesigned manifolding, fitment of a Cosworth Sierra intercooler, an increase in the maximum turbo boost from the standard 10-12psi to 20psi, and modifications to the ►

WESTFIELD WEASEL

ACCELERATION FROM REST (secs)

0-30mph	2.3
0-40mph	3.2
0-50mph	5.0
0-60mph	6.6
0-70mph	8.6
0-80mph	11.6
0-90mph	15.2
0-100mph	24.5
30-70mph	6.3sec
SS 1/4mile	15.2sec
SS kilo	29.0sec
Top speed	108mph (4800rpm)

ACCELERATION IN EACH GEAR

	Second	Third	Fourth	Fifth
10-30	3.3	—	—	—
20-40	2.3	—	—	—
30-50	—	3.4	7.1	12.8
40-60	—	3.0	5.0	9.8
50-70	—	3.5	4.4	6.1
60-80	—	—	5.0	7.0
70-90	—	—	6.6	8.8
80-100	—	—	—	14.5

FUEL CONSUMPTION — Test 52mpg

Average	58mpg
Cruising	60-65mpg

◄ standard Lucas-CAV fuel pump to provide more fuel at the top end.

This raised the problem of how best to demonstrate the engine's capabilities. Sticking it back in an old Ford Sierra just wouldn't do; however good the engine was, it would still have 2800lb of metal to lug about, and the performance would hardly compare with that of the ubiquitous Ford RS Cosworth.

A friend owned an old-shape Westfield kit car, and Wilsher reckoned that would really perform with 120bhp and 150lb ft to replace its 1600cc Kent engine. He made the request, and got the right reply.

Then the cutting and shutting began. The engine, heavy in a such a minimal car, needed to be mounted as far as back in the chassis as possible to aid handling.

A month or two along the way, Westfield Sports Cars' chairman, Chris Smith, got wind of the project. Well-known for his bluntness but never a man to ignore an interesting project, Smith speedily offered a 'proper' Westfield chassis, the latest wide-frame version built for the earth-shattering 270bhp V8 SEiGHT.

"The idea of a diesel sports car sounded a bit daft at first," he says, "but when I thought about it, I reckoned it might have potential in a few years' time as a kind of guilt-free sports car. We agreed to build a chassis for Richard Wilsher in summer last year, and we sent it off in September.

"I've really no idea about its production potential," says Smith. "It's certainly quick, and I think it's very easy to drive, too. If people want diesels we could certainly build cars or kits to suit them, but I've a feeling this one is still a few years ahead of its time. It does make a powerful case for fast diesels, though."

By November last year the car was running at Sword Automotive. The engine, mated to a wide-ratio five-speed gearbox from the Ford P100 pick-up, gave 110bhp at only 3900rpm on the rev counter, with peak torque of 150lb ft at 3500rpm. The figures were encouraging, but they also showed that the fuel pump, though modified for greater fuel delivery, was falling down on the job.

The engine would rev to 4800rpm before reaching a typical diesel 'brick wall' but at that point power and torque were both 20-30 per cent below their peaks, though still well ahead of the standard engine's. It went back to Westfield for trimming and finishing.

"We ran it first with the 3.9: 1 rear axle ratio we use in our Ford CVH-engined cars,"

0-60mph in 6.9secs — in a diesel

'There's a determined stirring in the engine bay, more a loud hum than a roar and the Weasel takes off in a most un-diesely way'

says Chris Smith, "but we found we were getting wheelspin in fourth when accelerating up steep hills. A 3.3 axle was still too tall, so we tried a 3.1, which gives about 23mph at 1000rpm in top and seems about right. From our first tankful of fuel we were amazed to get an average of 60mpg, even though for part of the time the car was on the short gearing, and everyone who drove it went for maximum acceleration."

ON THE ROAD

The idle is the main giveaway — that and the fact that some bright spark at Westfield has applied 'turbo diesel' decals to the rear body, right of the spare wheel. Otherwise the car is a latest-spec Westfield SE in red, almost too well-built to be a kit car and even equipped with a rev counter.

Twist the key and the engine rattles into life, puffing smoke from cold. The exhaust, half a Westfield V8 system with its outlet under the driver's ear, is surprisingly unobtrusive and engine vibration is obliterated by Ford's Sierra-spec hydraulic engine mounts. The whole thing seems remarkably civilised. You can be fooled at first into thinking the thing doesn't go at all. The throttle travel is extremely long, so you have to reach for the power. But when the engine's turning anywhere above about 2400 there's a determined stirring in the engine bay, more a loud hum than a roar, and the Weasel takes off down the road in a most un-diesely way.

To drive the car effectively, you have to think torque, not revs. Change up at 3500rpm, explore that long throttle travel and few cars with this level of performance will seem as effortless. On the other hand, in its present form, the engine only pulls hard between 2400rpm and 4800rpm, a smaller power band than many modern petrol injected four-valvers: the best of those work between 2500 and 7000rpm. Given the wide ratio 'box, you have to take care to be in the right gear at the right time. On the other hand, if you just want to trundle in the best family diesel manner, Wilsher's engine will operate smoothly down to 1200rpm in fourth or top.

After half an hour in the car, its power characteristics start to become predictable and normal. There's a little lag, but not enough to prevent well-timed power applications to boot the car out of corners. The heavy engine's weight seems to be concentrated far enough back in the car to keep the handling crisp. The turn-in is as sharp as a racing car's was five years ago, the cornering is flat, and you can provoke some entertaining final oversteer with power, if you've a mind. The car itself feels well enough bred and finished to be a proper production model.

We took the car to Lotus's Millbrook test track, to put it against the watch. It was driven by both our own Martin Vincent and by David Cox, a well-known club racer who campaigns a Ralt RT3 in Monoposto events and drove the car in early shakedown testing. In greasy conditions the car performed amazingly well, turning a 6.9secs 0-60mph time, running right up against its 4800rpm 'wall' at 108mph on the high-speed bowl. The figures on p55 are for dry-weather performance.

Wilsher: "For years I've believed in the efficiency of diesels"

Westfield with engine installed

A heavy flywheel wasn't needed after

T3 turbocharger instead of T2

Exhaust manifold adapted

Lucas CAV fuel pump modified

The old-shape Westfield kit car

A quick look at the RAC's national Class E (up to two litres, diesel) records showed that the Westfield Weasel could easily have found its way into the record books. Its standing quarter mile time of 15.2secs is a cool 4secs under the present record; with a time of 29secs it would have clipped 7secs off the present standing kilometre record. And there's more to come.

If finance were available (which it isn't) Wilsher reckons he could get the power up to 125bhp, and rev the engine to 5500rpm. More boost and a better injector pump would be the keys to that. Then you'd be taking 0-60mph in under 6secs, a 125mph top speed (well ahead of the present Class E record speeds) and a 30-70mph time to beat a Testarossa. That would really stop the traffic.

Wilsher insists his engine has barely reached the Stone Age of development. "There are obvious things wrong with it, and I know how to correct them." A decent phase one unit, he feels, would have 125bhp with, say, 170lb ft of torque and a rev limit over 5000rpm. "Sooner or later sporting turbo diesels will come," Wilsher says firmly. ■

Westfield ZEi

Now you can have fun in a Westfield without having to build it first

Price as tested £16,815 **Top speed** 107mph
0-60mph 7secs **MPG** 26.6

For Comes fully built, handling, performance, ride quality
Against Price, lack of refinement, poor attention to detail

ANYONE WHO BUYS A kit car has to be an enthusiast. They must enjoy getting dirt under their fingernails and scraping the odd knuckle, because they have to build at least part of the car themselves. But are there others out there who dream of owning such a car but would prefer to keep their hands clean? Westfield, among others, certainly thinks so. The West Midlands firm is the first low-volume car maker to get the green light to sell its cars in fully built-up form, so now you can drive away in a Ford Zeta-engined Westfield ZEi without having to so much as pick up a spanner. And that's good

PETER BURN

news for all car enthusiasts.

The catalyst for this happy state of affairs, of course, was the advent of Low Volume Type Approval (LVTA) on 1 January, which enables component car makers to put their cars on the road without having to go through the costly process of full Type Approval. However,

Westfield is only allowed to sell 500 ZEis per year and unlike Caterham, which will sell its Rover K-series-engined model in both fully built and kit forms, you can't get a ZEi in knocked-down form.

To get the ZEi through LVTA, Westfield has been forced to change its ways.

The all-new catalysed exhaust system is clean and quiet and runs under the car rather than along the sides, the front wings are bigger to enclose the suspension, the side mirrors are mounted further up the windscreen pillars, and the dashboard is no longer flat but a more shapely, moulded affair. New moulds have been built for the glass-fibre body, including one for the dramatic bonnet, which gains a massive bulge to accommodate the Zeta engine's fuel injection system. And the seatbelts have been transposed, with the upper mounts in between the seats and the buckle slots on the outside, so that Westfield can offer a rollover bar as an option (the conventional belts have to be mounted on the bar).

At £14,687, the ZEi isn't quite such an obvious entry point into the world of two-seat roadsters as we had hoped. It must now be judged against mainstream production cars such as the Mazda MX-5, which isn't a lot more expensive at £15,780, and of course you can now buy its most obvious rival, the superb Caterham K-series, over the counter for £14,995.

But surely the 1.8-litre 128bhp ZEi is in a different league from the 103bhp 1.4-litre catalysed Caterham? Perhaps it would be if they were the same weight, but they're not. With the Escort XR3i's hefty 16-valve engine mounted north-south in the front, the Westfield tips the scales at a portly 680kg to give it a power-to-weight ratio of 188bhp per tonne, compared with the 540kg Caterham's 190bhp per tonne.

As a result, the ZEi's performance against the clock is good rather than startling. It hits 60mph from rest in seven seconds dead, compared with 6.8secs for the 110bhp non-cat Caterham we last tested, while its top speed of 107mph (in fourth gear and limited by its aerodynamics) is just 4mph higher than the Caterham's. The torquey Zeta engine is more in its element when it comes to mid-range flexibility, but again weight is a handicap; the Westfield takes 8.6secs to get

from 30-50mph in fourth (Caterham 6.3) and 15.8secs to get from 50-70mph in fifth (Caterham 13.3).

Having said that, the ZEi always feels quicker than the figures suggest, and we know from experience that the Zeta engine gets stronger with some miles under its belt. Out on the open road the Westfield is responsive and eager, with strong mid-range acceleration and a lusty top end that is welcome if you venture that far up the rev range. There's little encouragement to do so, though; stripped of any sound deadening, the Zeta engine is noisy and coarse, while the Ford MT75 gearbox is disappointingly long-winded and clonky. Again, this could improve with time; another ZEi we drove was considerably more refined.

Don't expect any aural stimulation from the exhaust, either. The note is flat and barely audible above the chatter of the engine — certainly not a sound that makes you drop the hood simply to enjoy. It should keep the neighbours happy, though.

As you'd expect, the ZEi's handling is entertaining and capable. The car adopts a flat, neutral stance through corners that is virtually unshakeable on dry roads. If anything, the ZEi has too much grip — with optional 205/50 ZR15 tyres (the standard ones are 185/60 HR14s) it clings and clings rather than allowing the car to drift into controlled oversteer on demand. When it does let go, it requires a deft hand to catch it. The steering is quick and meaty, although it lacks some of the feel and delicacy that are usually found in abundance in such cars.

The quality of the ZEi's ride is a pleasant surprise. It's firm and tightly controlled, of course, but also remarkably supple. Sunken manhole covers are to be avoided, though — remember that you're sitting right over the rear wheels and you'll know all about it if you drop a wheel into a hole. The ZEi also feels ill at ease on very uneven country roads, bouncing and fidgeting rather more than it should.

The biggest flaw from the driver's point of view is

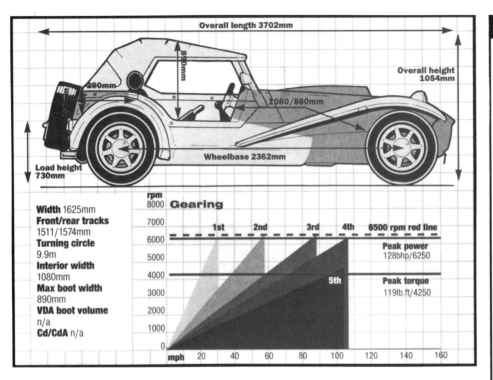

Overall length 3702mm

890mm

290mm

1080/880mm

Overall height 1054mm

Load height 730mm

Wheelbase 2362mm

	rpm					
	8000	**Gearing**				
	7000					6500 rpm red line
	6000	1st	2nd	3rd	4th	
	5000					Peak power 128bhp/6250
	4000				5th	Peak torque 119lb.ft/4250
	3000					
	2000					
	1000					
	0					
mph		20	40	60	80	100 120 140 160

Width 1625mm
Front/rear tracks 1511/1574mm
Turning circle 9.9m
Interior width 1080mm
Max boot width 890mm
VDA boot volume n/a
Cd/CdA n/a

Specification

Engine
Layout	4 cyls in line, 1796cc
Max power	128bhp/6250rpm
Max torque	119lb ft/4250rpm
Specific output	71bhp/litre
Power to weight	188bhp/tonne
Installation	longitudinal, front, rear-wheel drive
Made of	iron block, aluminium head
Bore/stroke	80.6/88mm
Comp ratio	10:1
Valves	4 per cyl, dohc
Ignition and fuel	Ford EEC IV electronic management, electronic ignition, sequential fuel injection, catalytic converter

Gearbox
Type 5-speed manual
Ratios/mph per 1000rpm
1st 3.89/4.73 **2nd** 2.08/8.86
3rd 1.34/13.75 **4th** 1.1/16.75
5th 0.82/22.47 **Final drive** 3.62

Suspension
Front double wishbones, coil springs/dampers **Rear** double wishbones, coils springs/dampers

Steering
Type rack and pinion
Lock to lock 2.75 turns

Brakes
Front 248mm plain discs **Rear** 241mm plain discs **Anti-lock** n/a

Wheels and tyres
Size 7x15ins **Made of** alloy **Tyres** 205/50 ZR15 Goodyear Eagle GSD
Spare full size

Made and sold by
Westfield Sports Cars Ltd, Unit 1, Gibbons Industrial Park, Dudley Road, Kingswinford, West Midlands DY6 8XF. Tel 0384 400077

Performance

Maximum speeds
Top gear 104mph/4628rpm
4th 107/6388 **3rd** 89/6500
2nd 58/6500 **1st** 31/6500

Acceleration from rest
True mph	Secs	Speedo mph
30	2.2	32
40	3.4	42
50	5.1	53
60	7.0	63
70	9.7	73
80	13.3	84
90	18.7	94
100	34.2	104

Standing qtr mile 15.7secs/85mph
Standing km 29.9secs/99mph
30-70mph through gears 7.5secs

Acceleration in each gear
mph	top	4th	3rd	2nd
10-30	−	−	6.2	3.6
20-40	−	−	5.7	3.4
30-50	11.7	8.6	5.7	3.3
40-60	13.2	9.0	5.8	3.4
50-70	15.8	10.1	5.8	−
60-80	20.9	11.3	6.6	−
70-90	−	12.8	5.8	−
80-100	−	18.3	−	−

Fuel consumption
Overall mpg on test	26.6
Best/worst on test	32.8/21.6
Touring*	30.9
Range	166 miles
Govt tests (mpg)	n/a
Tank capacity	28.4 litres (6.25 galls)

* Achieved over a pre-set test route designed to replicate an average range of driving conditions.

The figures were taken at the Lotus proving ground, Millbrook, with the odometer reading 740 miles. Autocar & Motor test results are protected by world copyright and may not be reproduced without the editor's written permission

Brakes
Distance travelled under max braking
Track surface damp
Anti-lock no

30mph	9.2m
50mph	27.5m
70mph	57.0m
st qtr mile (82mph)	86.4m

Fade tests
Consecutive brake applications at 0.5g retardation from st qtr terminal speed

(figures on the right represent pedal pressures)

	80lb
	60
	40
	20
	10
	0

Weight
Kerb (incl half tank)	680kg
Distribution f/r	50/50
Max payload	n/a
Max towing weight	n/a

1 Oil pressure gauge 2 Foglight switch 3 Heater switch 4 Water temperature gauge 5 Wipers switch 6 Fuel gauge 7 Lights switch 8 Windscreen washer switch 9 Main beam and horn switches 10 Revcounter 11 Warning lights 12 Speedometer 13 Hazard lights and indicators switches

that the side mirrors obscure vision dreadfully. The offside mirror neatly blocks out the road through right-hand corners, and even negotiating a roundabout can be difficult because you often can't see the kerb or a bollard in the middle of the road unless you lean well over to the left.

The view down the bonnet isn't all that appealing, either. The huge bump on the bonnet and the chunky wings make the car feel big and ponderous and half obscure the delightful fish-eye view of the world in the back of the chromed head-lamps. It lacks the elegance of the aluminium-bodied Caterham; certainly the ZEi still feels like a kit car.

The hood is a frustrating affair. The plastic bar that holds the front edge of the hood in place is fiddly and rather flimsy, while the frame is awkward to erect and the velcro strips that hold the hood to the frame are impossibly difficult to attach. And even if you persevere and get it erected satisfactorily, the hood still lets in lots of draughts and the occasional spot of water.

Getting in and out isn't too bad. The side screens won't swing all the way forward because the mirrors get in the way, but there is a handy ridge on the floor on both sides that prevents your feet from sliding forward as you lever yourself down into the seat. With the hood up, the handbrake on top of the centre tunnel can get in the way, but most people will probably welcome having it within easy reach (the Caterham's one is under the dash on the passenger's side).

The hood comes as standard, but you have to pay extra for a tonneau cover, rollover bar, leather seats and the big wheels. No provision is made to attach a cover over the luggage compartment, either, which is annoying.

We would be the first to applaud Westfield for giving the public the opportunity to buy this car off the peg. It's an honest and brave effort, and cars like the ZEi are great fun no matter how flawed they may be. But for similar money you could have a K-series Caterham instead. Need we say more? ■

Cockpit is a snug fit for two, but not unpleasant unless you have long legs. Steering wheel is dramatically offset to the right and the pedals are too close. Shapely dashboard is new; leather an option

128bhp Zeta engine, as seen in the XR3i, is rather coarse but gives fair performance. It's too heavy, though, hurting the car's power-to-weight ratio

Luggage compartment is big enough for a couple of soft bags, but there's no cover. Driver's vision is restricted by side mirrors and bonnet bulge, the latter needed to accommodate the fuel injection system. Ride is surprisingly good

Main dials have adjustable orange needle to indicate red line but are obscured by steering wheel

Handling is entertaining, but not as involving as that of K-series. Tyres provide generous grip. Pretty headlamps half-hidden from driver

Go Westfield

Rover's venerable V8 and Ford's new Zeta engine power these two high-performance machines, and both of them impressed *Mark Hales*

John Colley

ZEi has only a third of its big brother's V8 power – but a quieter exhaust makes it easier to live with – it won't frighten the horses so much either. As a fun car it's the best Westfield yet. 330V8, opposite, raises two fingers to aerodynamic design yet gets to 100mph in 7.7sec

Back in 1991 it hardly seemed worthy of comment that Westfield's V8 had taken just four seconds to struggle to 60mph – or that the trip onwards to 100mph took about the same again. Of course it was quick but then it was just another statistic in our performance files.

For the record and at the time, the 500bhp Ferrari F40 was still quicker, but only by a few 100ths, and the main item of note was that the Westfield could do it for around £16,000 while the Ferrari cost nearer to half a million. Since then, man's desire to make a competition out of all things – and the resultant marketing opportunity that the victor can claim – have muddied the testing water. Low-volume manufacturers had spotted *FAST LANE*'s name in the 0-60mph section of the *Guinness Book of Records*, and closer gear ratios and higher power outputs have

moved from the special order options list to be standard equipment.

Caterham even built a special car. Perhaps with an equal eye to the PR available from an impractical concept made even more so by obsessive weight saving, lurid paint scheme and no weather equipment, they nevertheless equipped the car with a first gear good for more than 60mph, even though the engine wasn't interested in anything much below 6,000rpm. We naturally went along with all that, anxious to claim our share of PR with another record This we duly did, as you will have read in last month's *FAST LANE*.

Then a magazine rival had a crack with a higher-spec Westfield V8. Yet more power from the venerable aluminium Rover engine, and a first gear ratio that made the magic 60mph equal 7,000rpm so that you didn't have the tiresome and time-consuming shift from first to second. Small matter that the Range Rover engine normally peaks at 5,000.

When we tried the car, the appropriately titled 300bhp SEight ran the Caterham to within a couple of hundredths in the 60mph contest. Not satisfied, Westfield have now installed a 4.3-litre Rover V8 modified by TVR Power to develop more than 330bhp at slightly higher rpm, and although it is certainly quicker to 100mph, it has perhaps lost a little of that car's simply unbelievable fourth gear performance. It is also slightly trickier to control the wheelspin from a standing start, so whatever is gained at the top end is surrendered to lack of drive at the bottom. Whatever,

62

Lower-powered ZEi shares the 330V8's fine handling capabilities. Thanks to its lower weight it is also a touch more agile when changing direction in a hurry. Twin-cam Ford Zeta engine sounds like an extractor fan but powers the car to 60mph in 6.7sec. Improved switchgear and instruments testify to continuing development of Westfield cockpits and a new hood system is on the way

it's still formidable, and Westfield has promised to freeze this latest 330V8 spec.

The latest monster Westfield can justly retain its claim to a number of other records. For just under £25,000, there's still nothing we can think of that will reach 100mph in 7.7sec from rest, or swallow up all the 20mph fourth gear increments between 40 and 120mph in 3.5sec or less. Not only that, the notion of the biggest engine in the smallest chassis ensures that it is still a comparatively simple matter to sidestep the clutch at around 3,000rpm and just go. The torque of four litres ensures that a few hundred either side hardly matters. It is only further on towards 7,000 that the masses reciprocating inside the engine assume relative weights of several tons, and the noise, fury and heat of the sledgehammer approach compares starkly with the science of high revs and electronically controlled, fuel-injected smoothness.

The 60mph first gear capability ensures that the remaining four ratios are closely stacked in the Rover Vitesse gearbox. The racer's preferred 400rpm drop as you flick the shift is good for producing adrenalin although the change itself was never the best even in its original location. Shortening the lever seems to make it even stickier.

Just for the record, and using some optional sticky Avon CR36 road rubber, we got to 60mph in 3.5sec from rest – leather seats, heater, windscreen, radio and all. With the standard 225 section Goodyear Eagles fitted, the car will now just beat the 3.9sec world record we set with the F40 in 1989.

Performance per pound, the 330V8 is distinctly unbeatable. The downside was the test car's total lack of social acceptability. The exhaust itself is not particularly noisy – the uneven waffle from the sidemounted silencers, each fed by the corresponding bank of four cylinders – takes on a harder bark as the revs rise – but it's all rumbly low-frequency stuff. The problem arises when you lift off. Air sucks in through the joints in the banana bunch exhaust pipes, unburnt fuel raining from the accelerator pumps in the four twin-choke Dell'Orto carburettors finds the oxygen of explosion, and the resultant fusillade from the silencers is like a mobile rifle range. Added to which the carbon metallic brake pads cried a demonic shriek as the speed slowed towards 30mph or so.

All this can make a maverick out of you without any effort. I was rumbling along some by-road when the exit of a fast-ish bend revealed a lady on a horse. Must slow down, give the beast a wide berth. Which involves lifting off the accelerator. *Crack...crack, crraack.* I dipped the clutch as the animal began to gallop sideways, filling both halves of the road. Better brake, and hard, or we would be adding impact to the aural assault. But the resultant piercing squeal only made matters worse. Simple rumbling sports car had suddenly metamorphosed into a monster killer Westfield from Hell.

This apart, however, the Westfield does most things surprisingly well. Bulky

Performance Comparisons

	Westfield ZEi	Westfield 330V8
Acceleration through the gears		
0-20 mph	1.3 sec	1.1 sec
0-30	2,2	1.8
0-40	3.3	2.4
0-50	4.9	3.0
0-60	6.7	3.6
0-70	9.2	4.6
0-80	12.5	5.3
0-90	17.8	6.2
0-100	29.8	7.7
Acceleration in fourth / fifth		
30-50	6.8 / 8.1	3.4 / 4.9
40-60	6.4 / 8.5	3.3 / 4.8
50-70	6.9 / 9.9	3.1 / 4.7
60-80	7.2 / 12.1	3.0 / 4.6
70-90	8.8 / 15.1	3.0 / 4.8
80-100	14.6 / ◇	3.0 / 5.1
90-110	◇ / ◇	3.2 / 5.2
100-120	◇ / ◇	3.6 / 5.6
110-130	◇ / ◇	4.3 / 6.9
Max Speed	133.1mph	130.7mph

◇ Car unable to gain these increments before the end of mile straight.
Performance figures taken at Millbrook Proving Ground in dry weather.

On the circuit, V8 is well-mannered

Tyre-warmers made and supplied by M A Horne, Verwood, Dorset. Telephone Mike Drury, 0202 822770

WESTFIELD 330V8 – WESTFIELD ZEi

V8 can now sprint to 60mph in 3.5sec – quicker than a Ferrari F40

225/50/15in Goodyears coupled with twin wishbone rear suspension put 330bhp in touch with the Tarmac without any fuss when the road is dry, and with easily controllable levels of terror when the surface becomes wet. Steering is accurate and the extra weight of the V8 engine has added some welcome meat to the steering feel. Push-on understeer is minimal and so easily countered with the right foot that it doesn't exist. Ride is good too, saloon car soft, although we didn't fiddle about with the dampers.

The circuit handling is also pleasantly well mannered despite the amount of power available. A few Avon-shod laps of Castle Combe race circuit turned a time of 69.5sec – a comfortable second a lap quicker than TVR's Griffith and a much easier task than I was expecting. Traction is excellent at all times; in fact it was quite hard to push the tail wide with the right foot; you need to boot it hard and early with plenty of lock applied. Reversing the action by gently removing the power recalls the tail. Neither is there any sudden and savage wagging waywardness when the power is suddenly cut while the chassis is loaded up with cornering force. All of which speaks volumes for Westfield's double wishbone rear suspension – a virtual duplicate of that fitted to the front end where ideal geometry is usually more important. The brakes, despite their public road protest, are entirely at home on the track.

Inside, the Westfield's cockpit continues to improve by the year. Trim is now much neater and the seats are much better to look at and to sit in, although they still lack side support. The biggest problem when going really fast is staying in them. Otherwise the seating position is good.

Westfield has since assured us that popping exhaust and squealing brakes are easily sorted, so if you have a need for ultimate performance and no luggage, the 330V8 may well be your answer. The company – newly housed in smart premises at Kingswinford – is rather keener to concentrate on what it sees as a more likely volume seller. Essentially similar in chassis specification, the Westfield ZEi uses the twin-wishbone suspension at each end, but the Rover engine is replaced by a twin-cam Ford Zeta driving through a

Granada-Sierra MT 75 five-speed all-synchro gearbox. There is a little more room inside because the Ford gearbox fits inside a smaller transmission tunnel, and items like rear-view side mirrors and improved switchgear and instruments, and a key-lockable bonnet, all reflect continuing development.

The major difference to the ZEi is the Ford engine. It is lighter and develops a little over one-third of the V8's power, but there's no doubt that this, together with its super-quiet exhaust and lower heat output, make it a good deal easier to live with. The 60mph-from-rest statistic, so important to its bigger brother, comes up in 6.7sec – easily quick enough to deal with most overtaking opportunities. Further up the speed scale, aerodynamics dictate that getting to 100mph takes four times as long as it does in the 330.

Somehow though, the Zeta is a disappointment. It seems hardly fair to berate the V8 for the noise it makes while complaining that the Zeta's hum is devoid of inspiration. But the whine from beneath the Westfield bonnet sounds more like an extractor fan than high-tech piston engine. The Ford gearbox meanwhile emits a series of clanks, rattles and whines. Hidden down in the tin recesses of a Granada shell, presumably you don't hear them. The gap between ratios two and three also seems less of a problem in the Ford.

Visceral appeal aside, the lower-powered car shares all its big brother's fine handling traits. Smaller and taller 185/60 section Avons cover 6x14in aluminium-alloy wheels, but despite the lesser tyre footprint, less weight under the ZEi's bonnet makes it a touch more agile, and it feels a little tauter while still riding acceptably well. Neither Westfield quite has the pointy steering precision of the Caterhams, but then the Caterham's semi-independent De Dion rear end doesn't put its power down so well as the Westfield's fully independent layout.

The ZEi is a fresh-looking, bright little car. Faster than it feels or sounds, it is designed to be enjoyed with the hood down on sunny days. At £15,000, it's not a great deal of car for the money, and the hood system still needs development – the Kingswinford factory assures us this is being sorted. The ZEi is nevertheless the best Westfield yet. ∎

Westfield ZEi and 330V8

EXTERNAL DIMENSIONS:
length 146in **width** 64in **height** 41.5in **wheelbase** 93in **track front/rear** 59.5/62in

ENGINE:
Four cylinders in-line, front longitudinally-mounted. 80.6mm bore, 88mm stroke 1,796cc. Cast-iron cylinder block, aluminium-alloy cylinder head, twin belt-driven overhead camshafts operating four valves per cylinder. Fully mapped electronic engine management with electronic sequential fuel injection. Exhaust catalyst
PEAK POWER bhp/rpm 128/6,250 (DIN)
PEAK TORQUE lb ft/rpm 119/4,250

ENGINE: WESTFIELD 330V8:
TVR Power modified Rover V8. 94mm bore, 77mm stroke, 4,280cc. Single camshaft operating two valves per cylinder via pushrods. 341bhp at 6,000rpm, 318lb ft at 4,500rpm.
Claimed top speed 150mph-plus, 0-60mph 3.6sec.

TRANSMISSION:
Five-speed all-synchromesh driving rear wheels via propeller shaft and Ford Sierra differential

CHASSIS:
Steel tube spaceframe, glass fibre two-seat open bodywork
SUSPENSION: front/rear independent with upper and lower wishbones, coil springs over telescopic dampers, anti-roll bar **brakes front/rear** solid discs
WHEELS/TYRES Aluminium-alloy 6J rims/185/60/14 Avon Turbospeed

FUEL ECONOMY:
Average on test 33.6mpg. Tank capacity 6.25gal

PRICE
BASIC:...£14,687
Optional 7J wheels and 205/50/15 tyres fitted to test car £261.25.
TOTAL:...£14,948.25

PRICE: WESTFIELD 330V8:
(test specification) including limited-slip differential and 225 section Goodyear Eagles ....
....£24,950 inc taxes

MANUFACTURER
Westfield Sports Cars Ltd, Unit 1, Gibbons Industrial Park, Dudley Road, Kingswinford, West Midlands. 0384 400077

VERDICT
Pleasant little open-topped car with good ride and fine handling. Ford Zeta engine lacks aural appeal necessary to compensate for impracticality, although car is quick enough. Whether the manufacturers like it or not, the Westfield will inevitably be compared with the Caterham-Rover, and at the moment, the ZEi just lacks that car's refinement of development in areas like weather equipment although handling is arguably better. Both cars cost about £15,000, which will buy you a fully-equipped Rover 220 GTi.

But a diesel? Sluggish, rattly, with oily smoke? That sort of diesel? Partly true, though certainly not sluggish. The Weasel does make a rattly noise when the turbocharged Ford engine is idling, it is true. There is a puff of blue smoke when you give the throttle a prod, and it smells like a taxi.

That is the price to pay for an incredibly fast, unbelievably economical sports car that loves the environment. Emissions are lower than from petrol engines with full catalytic equipment on board, so Westfield can advertise: "Green hooligans apply here!"

A drainpipe size exhaust terminates just below the driver's right elbow, bellowing defiance at the pansy petrol burners. With more than a few hundred revs on the clock the rattly diesel noise disappears completely, the last vestiges drowned out by the scanty muffler system. A standing start kilometre in 29 seconds doesn't really tell the performance story, because the Weasel is close to its top speed of 180 km/h, and has long since given up on acceleration. Much more remarkable is the searing acceleration from rest to 60 mph (96.5 km/h) in 6.6 seconds, and to 90 mph (145 km/h) in 15.2 seconds.

Even more impressive is the sheer torque of the four-cylinder engine. Modified by the west of England tuning company, Sword Automotive, the 1.8-litre turbo Ford engine is tweaked up from 75 bhp (55 kW) to 110 bhp (81 kW). That's nothing exceptional — until the engine is installed in a car weighing 650 kg, ready to go — but the torque figure of 203 Nm is quite outstanding.

Here, it seems, is a road-racer prepared to climb a mountain, in any gear. The only figures available are in miles-per-hour, recorded for a British television program, but they show 50-70 mph acceleration in fourth gear in 4.4 seconds, and (still in fourth) 70-90 mph in 6.6 seconds. These figures are quicker than you'd get from a Porsche 928 S4, an Aston Martin Virage or a BMW M3 Evolution. Make no mistake, these are the most important figures of all, in the range that allows the safest possible overtaking opportunities in everyday traffic conditions.

What is a Westfield? The marque started out in 1982 making pocket size sports cars in the image of the Lotus 7, but ran into trouble with Graham Nearn's Caterham 7

V8 engine rated at 280 bhp (206 kW), and this fearsome machine accelerates from rest to 160 km/h in 8.5 seconds.

The Weasel came from a project started by Richard Wilsher, of Sword Automotive, who happens to believe greatly in the future of diesel engines. Starting with the idea of installing his tuned-up Ford turbo unit in a friend's old-model Westfield, Wilsher finished up in

A Clean Set of Wheels

A LOTUS 7 LOOKALIKE THAT GOES LIKE A ROCKET, RUNS ON DIESEL — AND THE GREENIES CAN'T COMPLAIN

BY MICHAEL COTTON
PHOTOGRAPHY BY PETER ROBAIN

It's mean, it's green. It's the Westfield Weasel, a rakish Lotus Seven lookalike that accelerates like an Audi Quattro S2, but sips fuel at an average of 5 litres per 100 kilometres. How? It's a diesel! True sports car enthusiasts now turn faint and look for a chair. The world is filling up with supercars . . . McLaren F1, Yamaha, Bugatti and Cizeta joining the exclusive club right now . . . and sums adjacent to $500,000 are becoming common.

concern which holds the licence. Five years ago Chris Smith, Westfield's founder and proprietor, broke with tradition and designed what is virtually a new car.

The Westfield has a lightweight, but strong steel tube spaceframe chassis, aluminium sheet cladding (a principle used by Brabham and Ferrari for their F1 cars, until they couldn't resist monocoques any longer), and is finished with self-coloured bodywork.

The suspension comes from Ford's part bins, and the Westfield will accept most Ford four cylinder engines, or the ubiquitous Rover V8. In its ultimate form the Westfield SEiGHT is powered by a 4.0-litre Rover

partnership with Chris Smith installing it in a brand-new car. The engine is located about 6 cm further back in the chassis than usual to balance the car with the extra weight, and to make room for the intercooler. Ford's standard five-speed gearbox is installed, and a 3.1:1 differential was chosen for the best combination of acceleration and easy main road cruising.

Regarding the engine, Wilsher modified the cylinder head design to increase swirl and improve the combustion, fitted new manifolding, and increased the boost pressure from 0.9 bar to 1.4 bar. Typically diesel is the sudden way it runs out of acceleration just when things are getting inter-

esting. The needle flies round to 5200 rpm in the gears but at that point the engine just coughs and gives up, urging a swift snick into a higher gear. The tiny gear lever moves all of 4 cm on the way to the next ratio and there, just waiting, is another huge lunge of acceleration.

This Weasel is very addictive. It is extremely spartan by nature and the occupants sit either side of the Ford differential. It isn't bone hard, though, and the suspension is felt to be working on rippled, undulating surfaces. Rack-and-pinion steering feels almost direct, and the disc brakes (off the old Cortina model) are quite savage.

The first few miles, driven in heavy traffic and persistent rain, were far from pleasant, a reminder of how much refinement there is in modern designs. Later, though, it stopped raining as we headed west, from Westfield's Midland base to the Cheviot hills, and with little traffic to contend with the pocket-sized road racer began to make a lot of sense.

Many people, nowadays, would justify such an overtly aggressive machine just because it's a diesel, and does little more than sip its way through a tank of fuel. An independent, calibrated test indicated 5.42 litres per 100 kms overall, and best figure of 4.70 litres/100 kms.

The bad news is that the Weasel is, at present, just a prototype. Chris Smith and Richard Wilsher are using the first-off to gauge public reaction (which is very encouraging). Smith would want to turn the strong interest into firm orders — "ten or more" — before he'd consider putting the Weasel into limited production. The price would be very reasonable, though — less than £10,000 in Britain.

Manufacturer: Westfield Sports Cars Limited, Unit 1, Gibbons Industrial Park, Dudley Road, Kingswinford, West Midlands DY6 8XF. Fax: 44 384 288 781. Engine: Sword Automotive, Mark, Somerset. **M**

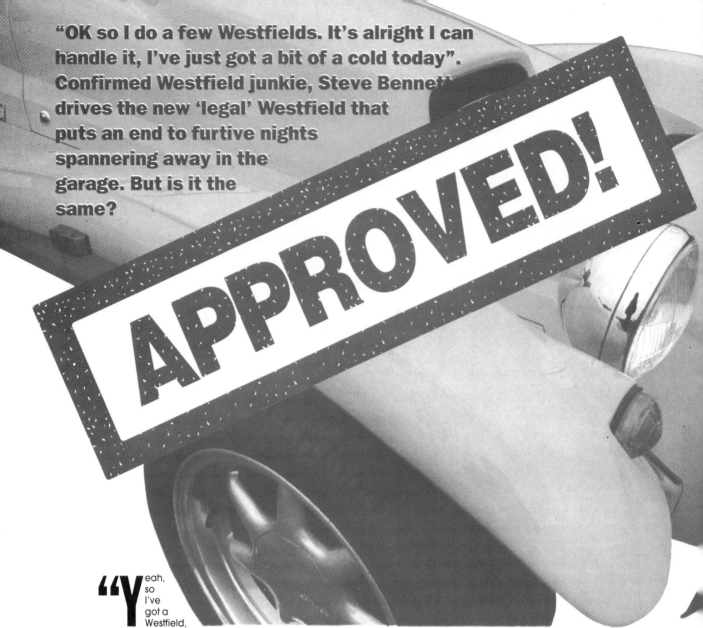

"OK so I do a few Westfields. It's alright I can handle it, I've just got a bit of a cold today". Confirmed Westfield junkie, Steve Bennett drives the new 'legal' Westfield that puts an end to furtive nights spannering away in the garage. But is it the same?

APPROVED!

"Yeah, so I've got a Westfield, it's OK I know what I'm doing, I can take it or leave it". A week later... "OK; I've booked another Westfield. It's not a problem; I just needed one with a bit more power, but I can handle it". A couple of months later... "Yeah I'm gonna buy a Westfield. So what, I know what I'm doing. I could stop if I wanted to, I've just got a bit of a cold today...".

Yes, I like Westfields and maybe I really will buy one, but can you blame me? The Westfield, and others of its type, are 'fun' cars. Driving a Westfield makes you feel like you're breaking a few rules. It's noisy, it's quick and you can build it yourself in the confines of your own garage. As despairing mothers say of their children's antics: "it's not normal".

It's all about conformity. Tazzing around in a noisy, self-built car is anti-social, but then that's the attraction. But in case you hadn't noticed, the 'suits' in Brussels have this idea that having fun is really not a very good idea and perhaps a bit stressful. The idea, presumably, is that we all lead very long and incredibly dull, bland lives.

Building noisy, anti-social kit cars is obviously deemed irresponsible and doesn't fit the image of a new united bland Europe, so don't be too surprised if, in the not too distant future, legislation stacks up against manufacturers - and indeed builders - of kit cars to render them both unacceptable and obsolete.

Grim predictions indeed, but all is not lost. Presumably in an effort to give manufacturers a sporting chance there is now limited-run type approval; a kind of scaled-down version of the type approval procedures which the major manufacturers have to go through. It's been operating in other parts of Europe for some time and is now an option in this country. This means manufacturers such as Westfield can now sell fully-built cars.

Westfield boss, Chris Smith, reckons that the writing is on the wall for the component car industry, but most of the manufacturers are too blinkered to see it. As far as Westfield is concerned, the future lies with fully-built, type-approved cars, and appropriately, the ZEi is the first limited run type-approved car on the market.

Even limited-run type approval requires some serious investment so it is perhaps not too difficult to see why some specialist manufacturers still have their heads stuck firmly up their... well somewhere fairly dark. According to Smith, type approving the ZEi has taken four years and cost the best part of £270,000. Clearly this sort of investment is only possible for a few specialists.

The new ZEi looks typically Westfield, but

● Still swoopy-woopy, yet subtly different; to obtain limited-run type approval ZEi has headlights and indicators integrated into bodywork; revised front wheelarches now conceal front suspension

PHOTOGRAPHY: JOHN COLLEY

nut and bolt torqued, has to be signed-off on the comprehensive build sheet. Type approval monitors could swoop at any time to ensure that the job is being done to the letter. It's time consuming and ideally the time taken to build a car needs to be cut by at least a day, but then this is new territory for Westfield and there is still much to be learnt.

THE ZETA FACTOR

The real story, however, lies under the skin. In order to fit in with the brave new world of type approval, the ZEi makes use of Ford's new Zeta 'world' engine in full 130bhp injected and catalysed form. Unfortunately, though, type approval means that the ZEi is severely silenced to just 77 decibels which, believe me, is boringly quiet. Yes the boring old 'suits' have certainly done their job in the noise department.

The Zeta engine may not be the best 16-valver around, but it is a good honest, tough unit with a reasonable power output. It also has the advantages of full electronic engine management and its standard - straight out of the XR3 - specification. This is an engine that will start on the button time and time again, and will comfortably sail past the 100,000 mile mark with little more than an oil ⇨

the changes are significant if well concealed. The headlights and indicators are integrated into the bodywork, while the front suspension, usually visible, is concealed by the revised front arches. These changes are subtle and nicely executed. The long snout now carries a fairly prominent bulge, necessary to clear the fuel injection system on the Zeta engine. You'll either think that it looks aggressive, or you'll hate it - opinions were mixed in our office.

These are some of the most obvious changes, but limited-run type approval extends way beyond this. Blunt edges and flat surfaces are out. You may build a kit Westfield with a flat aluminium dash, but for type approval the dashboard must be padded with recessed instruments. Inside the inertia seat belts must work absolutely perfectly. Even such items as the number plate surround must be chamfered and type approved.

At Westfield's impressive new factory, a ZEi car takes about three days to be hand assembled. Adhering to the strict build procedures demanded by type approval, every component fitted and every

SON OF SEiGHTAN

Well by now you will realise that I'm addicted to Westfields. You know how it is, they start you off on the soft stuff - Zetas and CVHs - but before you know it, you're on the hard stuff. God I thought I'd kicked the V8, I did honestly. But I was weak, vulnerable and they knew it. And it's not just the car it's the petrol habit too....

The Westfield SEiGHT is back and it's quicker than ever. In fact at the time of writing the SEiGHT is the provisional holder of the unofficial fastest ever 0-60mph time for a production road car at a mind-bending 3.45 secs. This is thanks to some minor fettling to the Rover V8 lump by JE Motors, pushing power output to 300bhp, and a revised gearing that will allow the SEiGHT to hit 60mph in first gear.

We had the SEiGHT for a week directly after the ZEi - a case of from the sublime to the ridiculous I guess. And yes, it is still the most outrageously fast road car this writer has ever tested. The definition of true fear, I can now exclusively reveal, is riding hotshoe in the SEiGHT with CCC's Miglia pilot, Bill Sollis, at the wheel. You may think that because Bill pedals a namby pamby fwd 1000cc Mini, then 300bhp might be a bit much but as they say: 'when you can drive, you can drive'. And so Sollis came over all manic and gave the SEiGHT death, his insane cackling almost drowning out the thunder from the pipes.

Previous to that the SEiGHT was punted to Yorkshire by yours truly. Being early March the forecast was for snow - and snow it did. What's the SEiGHT like in a blizzard? No problem: just stick it in fifth, drop the revs right down and it will chug along, quite happily, without a hint of drama. Left outside my parents' house for a couple of days, the SEiGHT had to be dug out, but it still started first time.

There was, however, one more sphincter-twitching moment. Blasting up a seemingly dry stretch of Yorkshire Moors dual carriageway, hard in fifth, I began to notice the odd momentary lapse of traction. Wheelspin in fifth! Black ice! Sheeeit! ■

● The mega-monster splash; CCC not only indulged in a spot of Seightanic snowploughing; we also got to take the 300bhp V8 Westfield to the test track. It rained...

Our car, with not a lot on the clock, was reluctant to give its all without a bit of a strain.

On the road the ZEi takes some getting used to. Not because it is difficult to drive, but because it is particularly precise. For the first few miles you find yourself oversteering and twitching everywhere, simply because normal saloon type steering inputs are just not necessary. Tune yourself in to the more precise demands of the Westfield chassis and everything starts to gel.

Comparatively the ZEi feels quite soft, certainly compared to the usual Westfield type set-up. The Spax dampers are, however, adjustable so you can be as masochistic as you like about ride quality. As it is the ride is surprisingly good and running it soft certainly improves grip on our typically bumpy roads. In fact if anything the ZEi is a bit mismatched on the grip/power front. In other words it seems to have more grip than it has power.

Soft also is the Zeta engine's throttle response. If you are used to the hair-trigger reactions of a twin carb set-up, then you will find the injection system on the Zeta engine positively geriatric. This, though, is inherent with modern fuel injection. Another factor is the Ford EEC IV management system that initially cuts into economy mode under full throttle. Expect a range of modified ECUs from the chip tuners to overcome this minor irritant. The standard Ford MT75 gearbox isn't a

● Above: Busy bees; new ZEis hand-built construction methods at Westfield factory (above). Unlike component kit sisters, ZEis leave the works fully built

change every now and again and a couple of new cam belts, dash of anti-freeze…

This is not an engine for tinkering around with so if your idea of fun is rebuilding your twin 45-equipped Crossflow every year, then this is probably not for you. However, Zeta tuning goodies are starting to filter onto the market and modified ECUs are bound to be popular. We would, however, recommend that you leave well alone (although we could understand if you ripped the insides out of the silencer) and let your local Ford dealer attend to it every 6000 miles.

THE DRIVING FACTOR

There's no getting away from it, the ZEi is quiet and while none of us would probably want to admit it (except me that is) there is a certain yobbish delight in howling along listening to the engine deep breathing. But there's no point in whinging about it, type approval requires it so that is that. (That's enough about rorty noises - Ed).

Anyway we can hardly condemn a car because it is not noisy enough (I said enough…) and there is plenty that is good about the ZEi. The first thing that strikes you is that it is a well-built car. It doesn't clonk or creak, the panels fit extremely well and the bodywork is immaculately finished. This is a solid piece of kit (ouch).

The ZEi needs its 130 horses because its solidity means extra weight. The Zeta engine, though, like many a modern 16-valver needs a few thousand miles before it gives its best. The word is that by the time the odometer has crept past the 6000 mile mark, then it is really starting to loosen up.

great help when it comes to getting the power down. To ease the passage of type approval the standard cogs are retained, with ratios naturally designed for saloon car use, rather than a minimalist two seater. The shift quality is long and a bit rubbery and can seemingly differ from car to car. However at least the relatively high top gear makes for reasonably relaxed motorway cruising.

These, unfortunately, are the sort of compromises that type approval inflicts. In order to meet the requirements at a reasonable cost, as many standard parts as possible need to be culled from major manufacturers. It is pointless for a company like Westfield to type approve its own engine, when Ford has already spent millions doing the job already, and besides the cost would be totally prohibitive.

The type of buyer that wants a highly tuned, razor sharp, street racer/weekend hillclimber Westfield, is not going to buy a ZEi. That sort of person would much rather be in the garage building one himself, which is why Westfield is first and foremost

the manufacturer of component cars. However, there are also a lot of people that would like to enjoy the minimalist sportscar experience without having to create it first. The latter also expect a car to be utterly reliable, and with its Ford running gear the ZEi should certainly be that.

● Main pic, left: No chance; Son of Seightan prepares to gobble up Bennett (above) in Zeta-powered ZEi

THE COST FACTOR

It's difficult to quantify the true value of a car like the ZEi. Certainly at £14,657 it is not cheap. In fact it is more expensive than the XR3 which donates its engine and drive train, but then that is to miss the point. The ZEi doesn't splurge off a production line at the rate of one every two minutes - it is completely hand-built. OK so maybe there isn't much to build, but it still requires a minimum of two days to be assembled in the factory. ■

Westfield Sports Cars Unit 1, Gibbons Industrial Park Dudley Road, Kingswinsford W. Midlands. Tel: 0384 400077

Wickedish
Small Sports

One is a pussycat, the other is as tricky in the wet as a Ferrari F40. Westfield's Cosworth-powered ZEi 220 meets the 200bhp BBR Mazda MX-5 turbo, while John Barker runs for cover

Photography Peter Robain

It's a picture of innocence, the standard Mazda MX-5. Sporty but unthreatening, almost cute. Drive it hard and you'll find an engine more willing than able and playful rear-drive handling. It's a lapdog of a sports car; Cert U, suitable for all the family.

But this is something else. What we have here is an X-rated version on very limited release — this is the only test you'll see of it. BHR (Brodie Brittain Racing) has taken its Mazda UK-approved turbo kit, uprated it from 150 to 209bhp, and fitted it to the car you see here. The 'regular' turbo is quick but this one is crazy; it's an MX-5 main-lining on boost, a car tattooed with 'live fast and die young', a car that will be found dead on a toilet seat.

It's the car you'd imagine the Westfield ZEi 220 to be. After all, a minimalist structure like the ZEi's should produce a knife-drawer of a car. Add the explosive Escort Cosworth turbo engine and you'd expect the resulting car to give you a short back and sides if you get it wrong. Not so; this 217bhp Westfield is a real softie.

It's the first limited type approval ZEi 220 (you can buy it complete from the factory), and the tight and neat installation of the stock 2-litre Escort motor has knocked off 10bhp and also created a very progressive boost delivery. Westfield isn't sure how, but is happy with the result and the way it blends with a chassis surprisingly free of sharp edges and more than capable of handling the power.

The car that'll cut you to ribbons is the Mazda. The 'Phase III' kit is not subtle, an effect you might presume comes from extracting 209bhp from just 1.6 litres of polished, ported and balanced twin-cam four. Power does arrive suddenly but boost is percolating through from just over 2000rpm and it's the short standard gearing that makes everything seem so frantic.

Slide down into the cockpit of the Westfield and you expect to be thrilled, but the Mazda is just like any other MX-5. You seem almost to sit on it, as if it's an eight-tenths scale sports car, and the muted exhaust note gives no clue to the terrifying transformation BRR has wrought.

Wickedish Small Sports

● Westfield on the chase — it's lighter, quicker and more powerful, but it's the Mazda with its fearsome boost that you want to watch

The first time it comes on boost in second gear is a genuinely startling experience. Passengers go silent or gasp nervously and even the car feels shocked by the ferocity; its pop-up headlamps ought to be raised permanently, wearing the same look of surprise as the people inside. The same controlled explosion rocks the car in every gear and only the rev limiter in top stops it going faster than 131mph — always assuming that the driver hasn't chickened out first.

The Westfield weighs 600lb less and is quicker still, but it doesn't feel as dramatic. Deceptively fast seems an odd phrase but sums it up. It too has a mellow, burbling exhaust note, in this case matched by a power delivery that is soft and well-rounded. Indeed, the Cosworth motor is much more progressive and user-friendly than in its Escort installation and sounds more refined, though that's undoubtedly because the rest of the car is noisier. Aural excitement is limited to the whistle of the

blower and the chuckle of the wastegate dumping boost on the overrun.

The in-gear acceleration times for the two cars are astonishing in two respects; first that they are blisteringly quick, second that they are almost identical. For instance, 50-70mph in fourth takes a mere 3.8secs in the MX-5, 3.6secs in the ZEi, while over the same increment in top the times are 5.2 and 5.5secs respectively. This is because the Westfield's superior power-to-weight ratio (253bhp/ton versus 190) is offset by the Mazda's sprint-like gearing.

Not off the line, however. The reason the two cars' 0-60mph times are similar is that the MX-5 was tested in the dry while the ZEi contended with soaking tarmac. Even so, it records 5.4secs for the benchmark, just ahead of the Mazda's impressive 5.8secs run. At 100mph the Westfield is stretching away, but it won't out-run the Mazda because of its out-house aerodynamics — 121mph is its limit.

The most satisfying way to drive the ZEi is in a gear higher than you'd expect, digging into the engine's reservoir of torque and surfing along on it. Perhaps anticipating a more rampant delivery, Westfield has set the twin wishbone rear suspension quite soft to soak up power spikes and keep the tyres in touch with the tarmac. It works very well, perhaps *too* well for those who enjoy a bit of tail-out action, because the car is surprisingly difficult to unstick, even in the wet.

The front end is also quite soft, which gives the ZEi a remarkably compliant ride but robs it of the razor-sharp reactions you get with, say, a Caterham. There's plenty of grip from the 205/50 VR15 Avons but the back end seems to lack a little initial roll stiffness and this takes the edge off the

'Dynamically, Westfield has achieved what it set out to do — to create a car in the fashion of the Lotus Seven'

quick and well-weighted steering's reactions.

At present, the ZEi uses the Ford MTX gearbox with a cut-down shift mechanism of Westfield design. The stubby lever moves quite well but it's not as direct and positive as the Mazda's — surely the snappiest manual 'box in production — and there are plans to replace it with the stronger Borg Warner T5 unit.

Considering their potential, neither car has the most reassuring brakes. There's no easy solution to the Mazda's problem, which is that it uses the standard all-disc arrangement. They're coping with almost double the performance and although they acquit themselves well, a beefier system is needed. It should be easier to make the Westfield's four-disc set-up more acceptable as the problems are simply too

● *There are just 1.6 litres under this MX-5 bonnet, but the engine produces 209bhp in frantic, breathless style*

● *Neat installation of the 2-litre Cosworth Escort turbo unit gives Westfield 217bhp, delivered amazingly softly*

● *Mazda's absolutely bog-standard interior has been left alone by BBR. Not even a boost gauge to liven things up*

● *Westfield interior pictured in a rare moment when it wasn't completely full of water. Nice leather, though*

much travel and not enough feel.

Dynamically, Westfield has achieved what it set out to do, which was to create a car in the fashion of the Lotus Seven, but without its frenetic, demanding nature. What BBR has created is its opposite.

In the dry, the Mazda is fun, but not in the same way the standard car is. The package of modifications that goes with the engine conversion lower it all round, stiffen the front end, and add a limited slip differential and five-spoke OZ alloys wearing 195/50 ZR15 tyres up front and 205/50s astern (Fulda Y3000s here).

Despite the wider rubber, the power steering remains rather light, demanding a delicate touch, but it's quick and accurate. And, oh boy, does it need to be. Turn-in is incisive and brisk but, as with the ZEi, the rear is relatively soft. Thus it takes a lot to

unstick the MX-5's tail but in second or even third gear corners, the engine is more than capable, demanding rapid doses of opposite lock if it's not to disappear up its own exhaust pipe.

In the wet, it's the trickiest car I've driven, bar the Ferrari F40. There is one similarity between the two, and it's the way the car snaps sideways instantly when the turbo whistles. On puddled roads you find

Wickedish
Small Sports

yourself listening intently to the pitch of the Mazda's turbo; if it sounds like Sweep on helium, a moment later you'll find yourself looking down the road through the side window, occasionally on the straights.

It's not a problem you can easily drive around either, because even in top on a light throttle, the power comes in with a bronco kick. BBR has plans for a two-stage boost control, which would undoubtedly help it stay pointing in the right direction and aid the car's longevity. Its owner has covered less than 3000 miles since his 15,000-mile car was converted and already the strain is showing. The gearbox zizzes in

the lower ratios, there's a slight rumble from the propshaft and the rear axle mountings feel as if they've done three times the mileage.

However, you wouldn't automatically choose the Westfield for a fast cross-country dash in the rain. To put it delicately, within a couple of miles you are at one with the elements, because the elements are creeping in just about everywhere.

Which rather makes a nonsense of the

● **This MX-5 is understated enough to bore the pants off car thieves, which makes it all the more shocking when the boost plays its trump card**

● *Snappy paint job adds to Westfield's sense of menace, but it's a surprisingly tame beast when it comes to putting all that power down*

optional leather trim (£900) fitted to the test car. It's well executed and stylish, the shapely seats and facia trimmed in dark blue with yellow detailing to match the exterior, but once the seats are wet, they stay wet. The simple, powerful heater keeps the chill off but also steams up all the windows, so it's best to go *al fresco* and ignore the pointing fingers and laughter. Caterham does it better, and offers a heated front screen.

The question is, what sort of people do the £22,000 BBR MX-5 and £19,950 ZEi 220 appeal to? The Mazda is easy. Its owner was looking for something special that wouldn't attract car thieves, which ruled out his first choice of a 911. One used MX-5, a trip to BBR and £10,000 later, he has a car that is as rapid as the Porsche and a sight more difficult to drive in the wet. Unlike the 150bhp conversion, the Mazda warranty is invalidated, but he

remains happy.

The Westfield isn't any more practical but buyers of this type of car know that. What they are getting with the ZEi 220 is a car with the look and feel of a past era with searing performance, a surprisingly good ride and fuss-free handling. Westfield considers this a good combination for covering longer distances (in good weather) and expects drivers who don't want a more demanding drive to beat a path to the door.

Impressed as I am by some of the ZEi's qualities, I can't help thinking that people buy cars like the Westfield for thrills. The manic Mazda, not so much burning the candle at both ends as applying a blow-torch to the middle, goes too far in the opposite direction, but you've got to admire its ability to silence passengers and dish up excitement. Live fast, die young. ○

PERFORMANCE		
	BBR MX-5	**Westfield ZEi 220**
THROUGH THE GEARS (secs)		
0-30mph	2.1	2.1
0-40mph	3.2	3.1
0-50mph	4.3	4.0
0-60mph	**5.8**	**5.4**
0-70mph	7.5	6.7
0-80mph	9.7	8.5
0-90mph	12.2	10.9
0-100mph	15.4	14.7
0-110mph	17.7	20.3
Standing 1/4mile (sec/mph)	**14.4/97**	**14.0/98**
Averaged top speed (mph)	**131**	**121**
4th GEAR ACCELERATION		
20-40mph	6.7	6.4
30-50mph	**4.9**	**5.3**
40-60mph	3.9	4.1
50-70mph	3.8	3.6
60-80mph	3.9	3.8
70-90mph	4.4	4.4
80-100mph	5.5	5.7
90-110mph	—	8.0
5th GEAR ACCELERATION		
20-40mph	10.6	—
30-50mph	8.4	8.2
40-60mph	6.0	6.8
50-70mph	**5.2**	**5.5**
60-80mph	5.4	5.2
70-90mph	5.6	5.7
80-100mph	6.3	6.9
90-110mph	7.9	10.4
100-120mph	11.5	—
Test mpg	**20.1**	**23.5**
With girlfriend mpg	25.0	28.0
Track conditions	Dry	Wet
Temperature (C)	7	7
Wind speed (mph)	4	15
Atmospheric pressure (mbar)	1005	989

Westfield's attention to detail has improved immeasurably in recent years.

A power/weight ratio of 292 bhp/ton is down to Ford's Cosworth engine.

Cabin can get hot, and breezy without sidescreens, but is 'snug'.

Westfield. The name conjures memories of a winter fortnight around 10 years ago, when I had access to a Westfield Seven. It used to shake its bonnet catches loose on London's poorly maintained road surfaces. Reluctant passengers had to hop out every third or fourth set of traffic lights to refasten loose clips. On one occasion, when travelling alone, the engine cover attempted a spectacular escape halfway along Deptford High Street, prompting an improbable one-handed catch.

A couple of days later, it ran out of fuel in rush-hour traffic. It had nothing so sophisticated as a fuel gauge; rather, before setting off it was prudent to dip something in the tank, and have a stir around, or to bounce the rear suspension to see if you could hear any splashing sounds. On this occasion, the volume of the splash had clearly been deceptive, and I had to push the thing for a mile and a half, only finally receiving an offer of assistance as I crested the apron of a filling station near Surrey Docks. . .

And the hood was something of an irrelevance (not to mention a near impossibility to fit properly, ie with all studs fastened). There were no sidescreens at all, so if it rained you simply got wet. If there should be night time precipitation, an inch or two of water inevitably amassed in the cockpit, its precise whereabouts dependent upon the angle at which one parked.

And yet I absolutely adored every minimalist moment I spent with it. It might not have been terribly comfortable some of the time, but it was fun. And beautifully balanced.

You could say as much about the latest ZEi 220, though were it not for the badge on the steering wheel you might never guess that it came from the same manufacturer.

Westfield has moved up several gears since the aforementioned Seven.

People no longer draw the tiresome, if inevitable, comparisons with Caterham that marked Westfield's nascent years. The marque has been around long enough, and is selling cars in sufficient numbers (as many as 400 per annum), to be taken seriously. Look at the modern new factory in the West Midlands. Or the company-backed one-marque racing series, which attracts decent grids.

Westfield has acquired a reputation f[or] mild innovation – witness the installation a one-off Turbo Diesel in a Z-type chass and its Suzuki motorcycle-engined Mi built specifically as a low budget racer – a has gained low-volume type approval for 'Z-range', of which the ZEi 220 is the curre flagship.

On paper, it's a seismic recipe: a 220 b Cosworth engine (turbocharged) in nimble, two-seater chassis based around mig-welded spaceframe (though, at 760 it's not a light car per se, even if it is rath more svelte than the 1300 kg Ford Escort with which it shares its running gear).

On the road, it is astonishingly tractab[le]

It takes a brave person to unstick a ZEi220 in dry conditions.

> *"People no longer draw the tiresome, if inevitable comparisons with Caterham that marked Westfield's nascent years"*

With a power-to-weight ratio of around 292 bhp/ton, you expect it to be lightning fast. But you don't necessarily expect docile manners to accompany claimed sub-5s 0-60 mph sprinting potential and top speed in excess of 130 mph. Even if circumstances allowed, it's doubtful that you'd *want* to drive at that rate: at an indicated 90, it felt as though your nose was somewhere near your ankles. That was, admittedly, without the sidescreens. Fit those, and your nose rises once again to its traditional position. It's even possible to have a conversation on the motorway, though it helps if both occupants have a vocal range close to Pavarotti's.

For all its ferocious speed, the ZEi 220 will pick up smoothly from around 1500 rpm in any gear. Torque peaks at 214 lb ft/4250 rpm, but there is a usable spread available.

And if you think its driveability is impressive, just wait until you experience its grip threshold. Accelerate into a second-gear right-hander, adversely cambered. Apply full throttle at the apex, and...nothing untoward happens. It just sticks and goes. So you try again, applying full power ever earlier, waiting to make a sudden steering correction at any moment. But it refuses to be unsettled. In the dry, the 205/50 Goodyear GVs could not be unstuck with a cocktail which built up, eventually, to about 90 per cent aggression, 10 per cent common sense.

In the wet, or on dusty roads, grip remains good, albeit finite.

The steering is as direct as any you will find this side of a kart, which helps, and the brakes were both powerful and fade-free. The drivetrain includes a limited slip diff as standard and a Ford MT75 gearbox with its well-spaced ratios but, in this application, a slightly notchy change quality. For this type of car, ride quality is surprisingly good, too. Cabin comfort is mainly let down by high temperatures generated in the lower recesses of the footwell, from which there is

"With the ZEi220, you are consumed by forgiveness in mere seconds"

simply no escape. (You also need an O-level in contortionism if you want to get in, or out, quickly when the roof is in place. Either that or to be an insect. . .)

Although the dash panel *does* now feature a fuel gauge, there are still a couple of throwbacks to horsedrawn technology. The indicators (operated by switch, rather than stalk) are not self-cancelling, and the combination of wind and engine noise makes it impossible to hear when they are on, should they be accidentally engaged. Also, the seat belt reels tended to lock inextractably unless the car was leaning slightly forward, a curiosity of which we have previously only heard tell on a Mk1 Escort. Luggage capacity is approximately zero (there is a little bit of room in the 'boot' when the hood is erected, but you have to remove the top to get in), and long-distance trips are severely compromised by a fuel tank capacity of only 6.25 gallons (with care, around 25 mpg should easily be attainable).

The latest spec hood is a simple, and suitably taut, fit, though the supporting frame had an unfortunate tendency to cross its legs and get itself in a knot, which took a minute or two to unravel whenever it needed to be retracted.

Such things brought to mind the old Seven. And you always forgave that its shortcomings within a couple of minutes of getting back behind the wheel. With the ZEi 220, you are consumed by forgiveness in mere seconds. Particularly when, as in this case, a pre-production car is involved.

There was a moment, however, when one's tolerance was momentarily stretched. At the northern end of the M23, after a lengthy drive, the revs died abruptly, flickered briefly to around 2000 rpm, then all power tailed off once again. Now there *was* a time when Ford's engine management systems used to overheat microchips when turbocharged engines ran in unusually high temperatures. The cure for that was to sit on the hard shoulder for 20 minutes and try again when things were a little cooler.

That proved to be the solution on this occasion, although the fault had a different source. Aware of the problem with the demonstrator, Westfield had relocated both radiator and intercooler on production cars, which reduced operating temperatures beneficially. When the same modification was carried out to L16 COS, however, the cut-out problem persisted. It has since been cured, following detection of a rogue fuel pump.

I got back in, and restarted. Moments later, I was again lost for any enduring criticisms. . .

Verdict

Go find a road, away from the beaten track, set a ZEi 220 loose and enjoy, enjoy.

No question, the ZEi 220 has some appealing habits: the sharp, responsive handling, steering that communicates in a hatful of languages, monstrous overtaking ability, docile low-speed manners, that supple ride. . .What reservations could one possibly have?

Well, how much does it cost?

Deep breath. You won't get much change from £20,000. And no matter how you look at its dynamic capabilities, that's still an awful lot of money for something with such overt practical drawbacks.

But reconsider a moment. It might run out of puff long before the average Ferrari (and, indeed, much other exotica). And it might not be as comfortable at common motorway cruising speeds as, say, a 2.0 Mondeo. *But*, in a real world devoid of 150 mph motorways, and strewn with truck-infested A- and B-roads, the ZEi 220 will have few peers.

A blend of race car handling and performance for the price of a Ford Granada (and a quarter of the cost of a 348)?

Makes sense to me.   **S A**

ENGINE	
Location	longitudinally front-mounted
Cylinders	four in line, turbocharged
Bore × stroke	90.82 × 76.95 mm
Capacity	1993 cc
Compression ratio	8:1
Valve gear	dohc, four valves per cylinder
Power	220 bhp/6250 rpm
Torque	214 lb ft/4250 rpm
Fuel	unleaded, 98 RON

TRANSMISSION	
Type	five-speed manual, rear-wheel drive

SUSPENSION	
Front	independent via wishbones and coil springs
Rear	independent via wishbones and coil springs
Wheels	alloy, 7J × 15
Tyres	Goodyear GV, 205/50 ZR15

BRAKES	
Front/Rear	discs/discs

STEERING	
Type	rack and pinion, unassisted
Turning circle	9.9 metres

DIMENSIONS	
Wheelbase	2362 mm
Front/Rear track	1511/1574 mm
Overall length	3702 mm
Overall width	1625 mm
Overall height	1054 mm
Kerb weight	760 kg
Fuel tank	6.25 gallons

PERFORMANCE	
0-60 mph	5.0s
Maximum speed	130 mph
Estimates supplied by Westfield Sports Cars	

FUEL CONSUMPTION	
Average for test	22.7 mpg
Government figures:	
Urban	n/a
56 mph	n/a
75 mph	n/a
LIST PRICE	£19,950

Starting grid for the fifth round of the Westfield Series featured 24 cars

Cheap *thrills*

Mark Hughes proves that participating in Britain's thriving sports car racing scene need not cost you a king's ransom

Going motor racing with your own sports car sounds like the exclusive preserve of the exceptionally well-heeled. In some cases that's true, but it can be done for a lot less than you might imagine. It's all relative, of course, and motor racing is always going to be more expensive than pigeon racing. But you could, for example, be sitting in the confined cockpit of a Westfield SE for a season for around £5,000. That's less than it costs to join some golf clubs.

The Westfield SE championship, for Westfield's Lotus 7 lookalikes, is the latest one-make series to appear in a British club racing scene that is littered with them. But this one is at the lower end of a cost scale which ranges from Citroen 2CV racing to Ferrari racing.

Photographs by John Colley

Mark Hughes: didn't take long to find Westfield racing a buzz

Instigated by Westfield's founder and owner Chris Smith, it provides close, cleanly-fought racing at reasonable cost to the competitor. On the evidence of the three races I've taken part in until now, I can thoroughly recommend it.

Westfield's roadgoing line-up comprises three variations of the standard product, ranging upwards of £14,450. It is quite possible to convert one of these into racing spec, but a more cost-effective method is to get the factory to build you a fully-prepared race car minus engine and gearbox for around £6,000 including VAT. Of the series' three classes, the least expensive and most popular is Class A, for which you need to get a fully-prepared Ford crossflow engine for around £1,700 and a matching gearbox for about £150. So your race car will have cost you around £7,850. After a season's racing you should be able to sell it on for £5,500. If you wanted to keep the initial outlay down you could, of course, buy a secondhand race car. The rest of your budget will be taken up by race entries (£105 a race for 10 races), a set of treaded Yokohama A088R tyres which should last a full season (£240) and, say, a further £1,500 for fuel on the circuit and getting to and from it. It is perfectly fea-

Racing throughout the field is close but contact is relatively rare

Two big Weber carburettors help give the old Ford crossflow engine enough power to make the 500kg Westfield feel relatively quick

sible to drive a Class A car – which is in a very mild state of tune and perfectly well-mannered – to and from the track, but that leaves you with no way of getting home if you prang it in the race. Most competitors prefer to buy a trailer and towhook. If you are a complete novice you will have to complete an RAC-approved racing school course in order to get your competition licence; this costs around £1,500.

If you don't want the hassle of buying your own car and running your own show, you could contest the season on a rent-a-drive basis. You just show up and drive, the rest is taken care of. It works out at around £800 per race, £8,000 for a full season.

A Westfield racer is formed from a strong steel tubing cage to which the suspension and aluminium bodywork are bolted.

the 1960s. It's tough, reliable and cheap, and will produce around 110bhp with twin Weber 40 carburettors. That is enough to give vivid acceleration in a car weighing 500kg.

Your Class A racer differs from a roadgoing version in a few key areas. The suspension's springs are shorter to give a lower ride height, there is a competition

Nigel Mansell might have trouble fitting in a Westfield cockpit

Because the Class A regulations stipulate a maximum capacity of 1,700cc, two valves per cylinder and a restricted camshaft, the most suitable engine is Ford's trusty crossflow, a pushrod design dating back to the Mk1 Escort of

spec roll-over bar, and most of the interior panelling is removed.

There are two other classes in the Westfield series. Whereas engines in Class A cars are restricted to roadgoing spec, in Classes B and C they can have

the full competition treatment, with bigger valves, competition camshafts etc. Bodywork can be altered to incorporate spoilers. Class B is for engines up to 2.0-litres, but still with just two valves per cylinder, and Class C is for engines of between 2 and 4-litres, including those with four valves per cylinder. Competing in these classes is more expensive as the engines need more attention and a couple of rebuilds (around £800 a time) per season .

Pembrey was the venue for my first Westfield race, my first two races, in fact, as this is the one double-header in the championship. On the track the Westfield feels like a small toy, it's as though you can do anything with it. Steering it, using the brakes, even pressing the throttle, none of it requires much physical effort. You're cocooned in a cockpit not much wider than yourself and this really highlights the feeling of the car being an extension of the driver.

It was while I was discovering all this that I first encountered reigning Westfield champion Chris Aspinall on the track. Although it was only qualifying, we became embroiled in a tit-for-tat dice, seeing who could brake later into the hairpin, try-

replacement from an old Escort. In the race the car was great and so was the racing; I become involved again in a superbly close and clean dice with Aspinall, eventually finishing ahead of him, but still behind class-winner Grosvenor. In the second race I spun while running second, again after a fight with Aspinall.

The next race was at Mallory Park where we qualified second to Grosvenor after another practice dice with Aspinall. In the race we retired with a misfire just as I was in the middle of an amazingly close three-car dice with Steve Kelsey and Aspinall for second place. I can't wait for the next round. ∎

ing to pressure each other into mistakes. It was great while it lasted, but it didn't last very long because my alternator destroyed itself for no apparent reason after half a dozen laps. The car came to a steamy halt since the alternator drives the water pump as well as charging the battery.

Although we'd done enough to qualify second to Westfield's development engineer John Grosvenor, we were left without an alternator for the first race. However, this predicament highlighted the friendly nature of the series – a spectator with a roadgoing Westfield lent us his alternator for the race – and how easy to maintain the car is; Westfield's Richard Smith simply drove to a scrapyard and got a

'110bhp gives vivid acceleration'

Sports car-racing selection

There are dozens of one-make racing series. Sticking to sports cars, here we pick out some key championships, graduating up the cost scale, you could take part in.

Budget of £8,000*
Aside from the Westfield series, you could instead try its direct rival, the Caterham Seven K-Series. This class is for Caterhams powered by Rover's 1.4-litre K-series engine and running on roadgoing tyres. A rough figure for an incident-free season would be similar to that of the Westfields at around £8,000.

£12,000-£13,000
With this sort of budget, a season of Caterham Seven-Vauxhall could be contested. Much more potent than the K-series, these 2.0-litre 16v Caterhams are among the very quickest of the one-make racers and producing times at some tracks that come close to those of the 450bhp TVR Tuscans.

£15,000-£20,000
You could do a budget-conscious season in TVR Tuscans for this sort of money, using an old car and not buying new tyres for every meeting. Tuscans are immensely powerful V8 beasts with far more grunt than grip and are not for the faint-hearted.
Alternatively you could contest a season of the Maranello Ferrari Challenge in the roadgoing class.

£35,000-£50,000
Very serious money territory. £35,000 could buy you a fully competitive seat in the Tuscan series, where you stand a good chance of being competitive in a very high-quality field of drivers.
Moving up to £50,000 would get you a similarly competitive seat in the modified class of the ultimate fantasy for many drivers; the Maranello Ferrari Challenge.

*The budget costs are based on race hire deals. Buying your own car and selling at the end of the season should be cheaper, but will mean more initial outlay.

Class C cars run with competition engines and modified bodywork

The scary SEiGHT: any number of ways of having fun and causing yourself mischief

And the **mark** of the beast was bright **yellow**, and the name of the **beast** was **Westfield**. The **SEiGHT** is seriously **quick** but this brutish force could **lead** you off the straight and **narrow**

A perfect

This car should carry a government health warning. If it fails to kill you with neck-breaking acceleration, it'll burst your eardrums with the violence of its V8, poison you with fumes or douse you in petrol.

The automotive assassin in question is the Westfield SEiGHT. The Lotus Seven-inspired body carries a 4.3-litre Rover V8 with anything up to 350bhp depending on the weather. It weighs just 1,630lbs. That's 480bhp/ton. Nothing short of a McLaren F1 can beat it on power-to-weight ratio.

It is an extreme machine. The standard wide-bodied Westfield chassis is clothed in a mixture of bright yellow GRP and black carbon fibre over the extra-wide wheel arches and cycle wings. The bonnet bulges, charred black side-pipes protrude each side and huge Avon Turbospeed tyres surround the 17-inch Tritech alloy wheels.

It's scary standing still but turn the key and the nightmare really begins. The four twin Dellorto carbs gulp in air and spurt jets of petrol like gasoline geysers. The exhaust fires an ack-ack barrage from each sidepipe and smoke drifts across the bonnet from the carb tops like a scene from *Apocalypse Now*.

And it never lets up. Even edging through town traffic in third, using the engine's tremendous torque, there's a

firefight going on at your sides. Every lift of the throttle brings shotgun blasts from the exhausts, prompting jumpy pedestrians to dive for cover.

But let's face it, with this amount of power environmental issues don't get a look in. There's no catalyst, you'll be lucky to get 15mpg and each mile is covered in a benzene haze. Who cares? There's over 300 horses to let loose.

Select first gear, build the revs to 3,500 and pop the clutch. The rear tyres light up and the hand of God punches you forward. As you snatch second the rear twitches to the right. Grab a quarter turn on the wheel to correct with power still on full and the Avons finally bite as you hit third, fourth and fifth. It's just brute force.

Westfield claims 0-60mph in 3.4 seconds, though on a dry Millbrook track we were unable to manage less than 3.8 and that was only by starting in *second* gear and blasting all the way to the rev-limiter. 100mph came up in a fraction under nine seconds.

A four-point racing harness holds you in the perfect position to be choked by fumes

Shotgun blasts from the exhaust are the scourge of pedestrians and cute animals

off-roader

FACT FILE	
Model	open sports nutter
Engine	4.3-litre 330bhp V8
Transmission	rear-drive, five speed
Price	£25,000
Rivals	Caterham JPE, McLaren F1,
	Bugatti EB110, a smallish rocket
0-30mph	1.9 secs
0-60mph	3.8 secs
0-100mph	8.9 secs
50-70mph in 4th gear	2.7 secs
50-70mph in 5th gear	4.0 secs

Recreating this sort of performance on the road would not only be remarkably silly but also pretty unlikely as there's such a fine line between going nowhere and going bonkers.

But figures don't tell the full story. Pick a gear, any gear, and the SEiGHT will cough, splutter and then spit you towards the horizon faster than anything you're likely to find on the road.

When they're gripping, not spinning, the soft-compound Avon tyres do a good job of holding the car on the blacktop and the brakes are strong and sensible. On smooth, dry roads you can barrel along quite confidently.

In slower corners the weight of the V8 will run the nose wide but a bootful of power sorts things out. Be careful though, a smidgen too much will send the rear sliding sideways.

There's hardly any weight over the rear so once the oversteer starts you've got to be very quick to catch it. If you're on guard it's easy enough as the steering is very direct, requiring just

over two turns lock to lock. But he who hesitates is lost. And too much correction has you fishtailing towards the nearest accident.

The solid Spax-sprung suspension can pitch the car off line over bumps and ruts and on country lanes and you have to make constant adjustments to keep on the straight and narrow.

You sit so low in the leather bucket seat that the sensation of speed is exaggerated as the hedges fly by above. But despite the flimsiness of the surrounding bodywork you feel surprisingly safe. A four-point Willans race harness holds you in the seat and although there's no airbag a sturdy-looking roll hoop sits behind your head.

You lie single-seater style with the pedals perfectly placed for heel and toe gearchanges. The clutch has little travel and the brake needs a shove but there's plenty of room in the pedal box.

Anyone could drive a SEiGHT but some wouldn't return. You respect its power but you've also got to question

it. At £25,000 you get more than your money's worth in performance, exhilaration and fear, but what about fun?

Because it is such a beast there are few times you dare use it to its full potential. The SPa we built may be slower, but it runs on skinnier tyres, it's lighter and it's just as yellow □

Story: Nik Berg
Photographs: Richard Newton

The Rover 4.3-litre V8 produces more power than you'll ever need or ever want to try

W is for... **Westfield**

GOING UP WEST

To build a **Westfield** kit car you need a garage, a good set of **tools** and a good sense of **humour**. To run one, you need exactly the same things. Or at least you do if the car has been **lashed** together by *Top Gear*

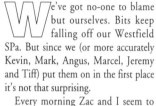

We've got no-one to blame but ourselves. Bits keep falling off our Westfield SPa. But since we (or more accurately Kevin, Mark, Angus, Marcel, Jeremy and Tiff) put them on in the first place it's not that surprising.

Every morning Zac and I seem to spend an hour in the garage repairing what went wrong the night before. Since we missed out on the fun building the car it seems we get all the fun of fixing it, instead.

In the first week our fingertight Westfield leaked like a sieve when it was caught in a thunderstorm and we had to remove the seats to get the sodden carpet out. Then the front off-side indicator fell off, it blew a bulb on the other side and we discovered that the headlamps were hopelessly out of alignment and you could keep fish in one of the rear lights.

But by far the most annoying fault was a blowing fuse which meant the reversing and brake lamps didn't work.

At first we thought we'd traced the problem to that water-logged rear light lens. We drained it out and dried the connections but the problem wasn't solved. After more head scratching we popped the car down to our friends at Supreme Autos (they came second in the build-a-Westfield race) and we managed to trace the fault to a dodgy connection in the wiring loom.

While there we also discovered a rocker cover gasket leak, a sump leak and a shiny Snap-On socket still attached to the gearbox. Oops.

The next day the other front indicator fell off and the same fuse blew again so Zac popped it in to another friendly garage, Bal & Co in Letchworth, who pointed out that there was so much slack in the wiring loom that it was chafing and shorting out against the differential. They kindly fixed it

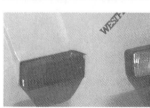

Pedestrians stop to ask why the word Sock is written on the bonnet. We could breed fish in the rear lamps after a rain storm, but not in the front indicators because they don't stay on long enough

and replaced a couple of missing exhaust manifold bolts for £21.50.

For a time all was well and we racked up 1,000 miles in a week, all of it top down and side-screens off, bugs in the teeth.

It's the only way to drive the car because with the sidescreens on your view is restricted and so is your elbow room. Taller drivers moan of bashing their bits on the screens every time they take a corner. For long, fast journeys they do have to go back on, though, as the buffeting becomes so severe you can hardly see.

So far the roof has only been on once and since it leaked so badly we haven't bothered since.

Around town, the Westfield is dwarfed by all other traffic, but you don't feel vulnerable down there. It's so loud and so yellow that other drivers can't fail to notice you. Pedestrians and cyclists love to read the signatures on

the bonnet but are invariably disappointed to find out that they don't belong to famous racing drivers, just the *Top Gear* team.

City pollution doesn't go down well either. After half an hour in London traffic you emerge looking like a chimney sweep from *Mary Poppins*.

Unlike most kit car builders we were able to send ours back to Westfield for its 1,000-mile first oil change when they also changed the nasty rubber gaiters round the gearknob and handbrake for more fetching leather jobs.

Although barely a day has gone by without work being needed on the car it is proving very popular in the office, especially after it proved its worth at Bruntingthorpe (see A – p78).

Despite being roundly thrashed, the Westfield was the only car not to wreck its tyres during our day of advanced Tiffery. On the mile-long straight it recorded a windy and rather ambitious

125mph on the speedo – we reckon it over-reads by a good 15 per cent or more. We've yet to figure the car but Westfield's claim of 0-60mph in six seconds seems plausible.

Through the corners the Westy did as best it could, but the skinny Avon tyres meant it was always fighting for grip. Its quick steering made it the perfect car for the slalom test, though. It was a fine balance between speed and grip and, as a result, several of the favourites (Marcel, Nat, Angus, Zac, Tiff) toppled over.

But the car never failed until it got home, when yet another blown fuse caused it to overheat spectacularly in a traffic jam.

And as if that wasn't enough, Zac tore the sump off on a gate stop and it had to be replaced (thanks again, Supreme) with a shallower one.

There's no doubt that the Westfield has been the most problematic car

we've had on *Top Gear*, but since most of those problems have been our fault, either through our shoddy build or through accidents, we can't complain.

Especially now that the sun's out. Even the road test department cynics, who sniggered every time something went wrong, are itching to get into it.

Let them have their fun. I know that as soon as autumn arrives and they discover there's no heater, the keys will be back in my pocket.

Nik Berg

WEST FIGURES	
Price	£8,500 (complete kit)
Engine	1.7-litre Ford Crossflow with twin Webers and fast road cam, 120bhp
Performance	0-60mph 6 secs, 110mph
Mileage	1,876
Test mpg	23.6
Faults	Blown fuses, iffy wiring loom, leaky hood, blown bulbs, leaking sump, leaky gasket, bashed sump (accident)
Costs to date	£57.49

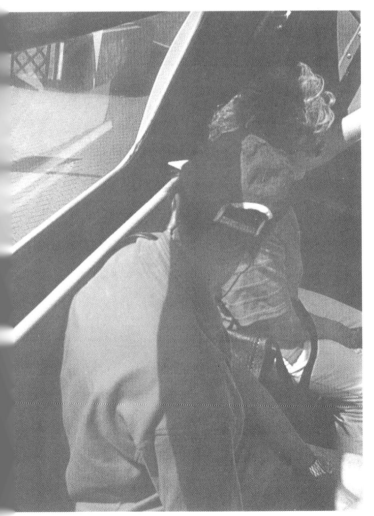

This is an official London

Photography: Jim Forrest

The only way to drive the Westfield is top down, doors off, even if you do end up looking like a rather sooty extra from *Mary Poppins*. The engine's great but a bit leaky around the sump and rocker cover

WESTFIELD 220

> **"Amazing performer"**
> 220 – Top Gear Magazine

WESTFIELD 220	
Engine	Ford Cosworth DOHC 16v
Cylinders	Four in line
Displacement	1993cc
Bore and stroke	90.82mm x 76.95mm
Compression ratio	8:1
Fuel	Super unleaded only
Exhaust	Three way catalyst
Valves	Four per cylinder DOHC
Max. power	220bhp @ 6250 rpm
Max. torque	290 Nm @ 4250 rpm
Gearbox	Borg Warner T5 – 5 Speed
Speed per 1000 rpm	23.08 mph (3.62 diff)
0-60 mph	4.7 seconds
Top speed	140 mph plus
Steering	Rack and pinion
Brakes	Disc brakes all round
Wheels	7 x 15 alloy
Tyres	205 x 50 x 15
Fuel tank capacity	6.25 gallons

> **"Throttle response in the low to middle speed ranges is swift and eager"**
> 130 – The Independent

The Westfield 220 and 130 are built to the exacting requirements of the Government Vehicle Certification Agency low volume type approval, fully meet current emission standards and can be registered on a current registration number.

Both cars are comprehensively equipped, factory built, modern, high performance sports cars incorporating the best traditional values backed up by a full twelve

> **"A blend of race car handling and performance for the price of a Ford Granada (and a quarter of the cost of a 348)"**
> 220 – Motor Sport

month warranty and a factory service scheme. The 220 and 130 have identical body and chassis components with adjustable independent front and rear suspension and are finished to the same exceptionally high standard. The 220 features the legendary Ford Cosworth 2 litre, overhead cam, fuel injected, turbo engine developing 220bhp and is

WESTFIELD 130	
Engine	Ford Zetech DOHC 16v
Cylinders	Four in line
Displacement	1796cc
Bore and stroke	80.6mm x 88.0mm
Compression ratio	10:1
Fuel	95 Octane unleaded only
Exhaust control	Three way catalyst
Valves	Four per cylinder DOHC
Max. power	130bhp @ 6250 rpm
Max. torque	162 Nm @ 4250 rpm
Gearbox	Ford MT75 – 5 Speed
Speed per 1000 rpm	23.08 mph (3.62 diff)
0-60 mph	6.5 seconds
Top speed	118 mph
Steering	Rack and pinion
Brakes	Disc brakes all round
Wheels	7 x 15 alloy
Tyres	205 x 50 x 15
Fuel tank capacity	6.25 gallons

WESTFIELD 130

fitted with ventilated front disc brakes and a limited slip differential, all combining into a unique package of exceptional performance, style and high speed fun. The 130 is fitted with a 1.8 litre fuel injected twin cam engine and is specified for relaxed fun motoring.

Both models have catalytic converters, a five speed gear box,

full weather equipment (excludes tonneau cover), heater and full instrumentation as standard. The body design differs from other Westfields to comply with type approval standards and incorporates the classic swept long front wings that are a hallmark of our traditional styling. Racing cycle front wings are available as an option at no extra cost.

WESTFIELD SEiGHT

In the super car league, the Seight has not only created a division of its own, it has re-written the rules! The combination of a superbly nimble and precise handling chassis with the light weight, power and immense torque of the Rover V8 engine has produced a car of legendary proportions that can out-perform all but the most elite, exotic and expensive machines from those such as McLaren and Ferrari and at less

than a tenth of the price.

With the smooth, continuous and never ending delivery of power, racing car handling, precise steering and powerful brakes the Seight is enormous fun to drive. In traffic, the V8 burbles happily along, hour after hour, but on the open road is ready to spring to life with instant, meteoric acceleration and an exhaust note that is only rivalled by the legendary Harley

Davidson, all guaranteed to produce an off the scale grin factor. And to cap it all, the Seight, like all other Westfields, is easy and inexpensive to insure.

Two models of the Seight are available, the *Euro* and the *Club*. The *Euro* is manufactured to the same exacting standards as the 130 and 220 to meet Government Vehicle Certification Agency requirements and is only supplied as a fully built car. The *Club* may be supplied as a factory fully built car or in easy to build component form for home completion. It shares the same mechanical

components as the *Euro* but has different body work, is lighter and more suitable for those with limited budgets or competition in mind.

Both models are fitted with a fuel injected Rover 3.9 litre V8 engine developing 207bhp equipped with a catalytic converter to meet current emission standards and can be registered on current registration numbers. The specification also includes a five speed gearbox, limited slip differential, ventilated front disc brakes, independent rear suspension and full weather equipment (excludes tonneau). Both models are only available with cycle front wings.

WESTFIELD 1600

WESTFIELD 1600	
Engine	Ford CVH
Cylinders	Four in line
Displacement	1597cc
Bore and stroke	79.96mm x 79.52mm
Compression ratio	9.5:1
Fuel	95 Octane unleaded
Exhaust system	Stainless steel
Valves	Two per cylinder SOHC
Max. power	105bhp @ 6000 rpm
Max. torque	132 Nm @ 4000 rpm
Gearbox	Ford Type 9 – 5 Speed
Speed per 1000 rpm	21.66 mph (3.9 diff)
0-60 mph	6.3 seconds
Top speed	108 mph
Steering	Rack and pinion
Brakes	Disc brakes all round
Wheels	6 x 14 alloy
Tyres	185 x 60 x 14
Fuel tank capacity	6.25 gallons

The Westfield 1600 is supplied as a factory built car or in easy to build component form with the further option of stage by stage modules to spread the cost and represents exceptional value in the mid-performance range.

The 1600 has identical chassis, suspension, bodywork and interior trim to its bigger engine stablemate the 1800. It is fitted with the Ford 1.6 litre CVH single cam engine developing 105bhp with twin weber 40 carburettors and the classic 4 into 1 side exhaust system.

"There are plenty of expensive whizz bang sports cars out there that are dead from the tyres up. But not this Westfield. It's got soul."

"A terrific car and great value"
1600 – Richard Simpson
Guardian Weekend

To help those with limited budgets we have equipped the car with remanufactured engine, gearbox and differential units. This effects a considerable saving at no disadvantage as all the units are fully rebuilt to the highest standard and are covered by a full 12 month guarantee.

As the vehicle is not equipped with catalytic converter and has re-manufactured components it will be registered on 'Q' number plates. If your car is supplied fully built, we will deal with all registration formalities. If you build a component car then we will check the car on completion for a nominal charge and help you with the registration formalities.

WESTFIELD 1800

The Westfield 1800 is available as a fully built car or in easy to build component form with the further option of stage by stage modules to spread the costs. The car is based upon the renowned Westfield SEI of which over 3000 have been sold representing the highest testimony to the Westfield philosophy of affordable excellence. Over a period of 13 years we have continuously improved and developed all aspects of the car to its current high standard and it is our most popular model. The 1800 is built with all new components, has fully independent all round suspension, a five speed gearbox and is fitted with the Ford 1.8 Zetec 16 valve twin cam engine developing 130bhp, with catalytic converter and comes with full weather equipment (except Tonneau cover). In component form the modules

WESTFIELD 1800	
Engine	Ford Zetech DOHC 16v
Cylinders	Four in line
Displacement	1796cc
Bore and stroke	80.6mm x 88.0mm
Compression ratio	10:1
Fuel	95 Octane unleaded only
Exhaust control	Three way catalyst
Valves	Four per cylinder DOHC
Max. power	130bhp @ 6250 rpm
Max. torque	162 Nm @ 4250 rpm
Gearbox	Ford MT75 – 5 Speed
Speed per 1000 rpm	23.08 mph (3.62 diff)
0-60 mph	6.5 seconds
Top speed	118 mph
Steering	Rack and pinion
Brakes	Disc brakes all round
Wheels	6 x 14 alloy
Tyres	185 x 60 x 14
Fuel tank capacity	6.25 gallons

are arranged in an easy to follow logical build sequence, each module containing all the parts neccessary for that build stage. Full instructions and a build manual are provided and a factory help line is available six day a week. Building a modular component car does not require any special equipment and is well within the reach of the average enthusiast. Average build time is not more than 100 hours. On completion, for a nominal charge, we will undertake a factory inspection of your car to ensure that all is well. As all new components are used and the engine meets current emission standards it will be accepted for registration on a current registration number. If we build the car for you it will be supplied registered.

The factory built car is covered by a full Westfield 12 months warranty. All parts supplied by us for the component car are also covered by an exchange replacement warranty scheme for 12 months. The Ford engine and gearbox have an unlimited mileage Ford guarantee and service and repairs are available at all Ford dealerships.

A *Special Equipment* option is available and features a 4.6 litre, fuel injected, 300bhp engine, modified suspension and brakes, racing type seats and safety belts and road legal racing compound tyres. The SEiGHT *Special Equipment* is only available as a factory built car.

"Ferrari F40 beating acceleration"
Encyclopedia of Super Cars

"Sounds like thunder, goes like lightning"
Autocar

WESTFIELD SEiGHT	
Engine	Rover V8
Cylinders	Eight
Displacement	3950cc
Bore and stroke	94.04mm x 71mm
Compression ratio	9.35:1
Fuel	95 Octane unleaded
Exhaust control	Two-three way catalyst
Valves	Two per cylinder
Max. power	200bhp @ 4750 rpm
Max. torque	318.8 Nm @ 2600 rpm
Gearbox	Rover R380 5 speed
Speed per 1000 rpm	25.45 mph (3.38 differential)
0-60 mph	4.3 seconds
Top speed	138 mph
Steering	Rack and pinion
Brakes	Disc brakes all round
Wheels	7 x 15 alloy
Tyres	205 x 50 x 15
Fuel tank capacity	11 gallons

Information, specifications, dimensions and general data contained in this publication is given for guidance only and may be subject to change without notice.

PETER MOSS PHOTOGRAPHY

The WESTFIELDs

The not-exactly-a-Lotus-Seven company will build you an SPa four or a V-8 Seight

BY PETER EGAN
PHOTOS BY GUY SPANGENBERG

IT'S HARD TO say whether the original Lotus Seven, as penned by Colin Chapman, is an actual car design or simply a state of mind that keeps surfacing over and over again through automotive history.

The concept is simple: Build a bridge between two sets of wheels, make a place for an engine and two people, add bodywork and fenders, grudgingly. Keep it light and low, and blow the doors off people who think a car is some kind of commemorative monument to itself rather than a tool for speed.

We see this theme all the way from ancient stripped-down Model T raceabouts to the homebuilt road-racing specials of the early Fifties. Chapman, of course, went beyond the backyard stage by mass-producing his feisty little roadster and tidying up its lines and proportions so that it became a handsome, classical shape in its own right—a monument to itself as well as a tool for speed.

When Chapman lost interest in building the Seven, he handed the production rights in 1973 to a Lotus dealer named Graham Nearn, who now builds the Caterham Seven along close-to-original lines, but the design has been copied over the years, to varying degrees of faithfulness, by dozens of other companies.

One of those companies, Westfield Sports Cars, Ltd., of Kingswinford, West Midlands, began in 1982 to build Lotus Eleven and Seven copies that hit a little too close to home for Caterham cars, which won a cease and desist order against Westfield's founder, Chris Smith, forcing Westfield to metamorphose its designs further away from the original.

So what we have here are a pair of Seven-like cars that can't call themselves Sevens or look exactly like Chapman's original design. One, called the "SPa" model, is powered by a 4-cylinder Ford Kent engine, essentially a Formula Ford engine with two Webers, bored out from 1600 to 1700 cc. The other is called the "Seight" (Seven with eight, get it?) with a 250-bhp (estimated) 3.6-liter aluminum Buick V-8 under its bulging bonnet.

All cars are now imported and built to turn-key readiness by an expatriate Brit named Bob Yarwood, who runs his shop in the Northwest (Westfield Cars of North America, Yarwood Industrial Estate, 83485 North Pacific Highway, Creswell, Ore. 97426; telephone [503] 895-3000, fax [503] 895-3400). Bob is a mechanical engineer who once did contract work for Rolls-Royce Aircraft division, but left to pursue his passion for vintage-car racing, restoration and engine building.

The turn-key cars come titled and ready to drive. Bob says their 1967 and earlier engines make it possible to title the cars in Oregon as 1996 Westfields or in California, for instance, as 1962 Buicks or 1967 Ford Cortinas, depending on the engine choice for the particular model.

Yarwood stresses that Westfield now sells cars in kit form under duress only for off-highway use (road racing, autocrossing) and, even then, only to engineers or other qualified builders. Otherwise, the entire car—including engine—is built in what he calls "a converted chicken coop" on his farm in Oregon. There are, he stresses, no other legitimate American dealers.

He presented us with both current U.S. models to test: the 4-cylinder SPa ($21,000 base price, $21,995 with up-

■ The SPa is Ford-powered, lithe and snarly, especially to the driver, whose left ear isn't all that far from the noise. In fact, in a Westfield, you're never all that far from *anything*.

grade kit, as tested) and the V-8-powered Seight ($29,950).

To distance itself from the copyrighted Lotus/Caterham look, Westfield has given the cars a single-piece fiberglass body wrap that forms the sides, rear fenders and back end of the car, rather than aluminum panels riveted to the mild steel tubular spaceframe, with separate fiberglass fenders. Beneath the fiberglass, there are still 12-gauge aluminum side and floor panels, for strength and rigidity, but the glass outer body is held in place with just 26 rivets and has no real effect on chassis stiffness. Front fenders bolt on separately.

The Seight has a similar chassis, but uses heavier-gauge tubing in critical areas, such as suspension mounting points, and a bit more triangulation. Track is also 9.0 in. wider at the rear and 7.0 in. at the front, though the engine bay itself did not have to be widened to accept the V-8. Track was increased partly to accommodate the larger tires, but mostly to achieve handling balance on what is simply a faster and more powerful car.

The Seight has cycle-type fenders at the front and detachable fenders at the rear, both made with carbon-fiber inserts to prevent, as Yarwood says, "throwing a stone straight through the wing at 150 mph." The clamshell-style front fenders of the SPa are not available on the V-8 car, he adds, because their width would cause too much aerodynamic lift at speed.

Other visual differences between the two cars are the large power bulge and the airscoop in the hood, which accommodates the V-8's K&N air filter. It also has seats with built-in headrests, which the 4-cylinder car does not, though clip-in headrests are available. Footwells are also slightly narrower in the Seight, because of engine and transmission width, and the V-8

has twin external exhaust collectors and sidepipes.

While the V-8 offers gobs of performance (which we'll get into in a moment), the 4-cylinder SPa was the more popular daily driver around our office, mostly on the basis of handling finesse, ease of driving and overall balance. Nearly everyone also thought it the handsomer version, though the Seight can be said to have its own hot-rod/track-roadster charm.

Though it has only 1700 cc of displacement, the SPa is still a stunning performer, as 4-cylinder Lotus Sevens with well-built engines have always been. It leaps off the line as if weightless, rips up through its five closely spaced ratios with a satisfying snarl and maneuvers through traffic like a cat. The Ford Sierra gearbox shifts with a quick, precise click; the 4-wheel disc brakes are powerful and linear; and the pedals are nicely spaced, if a bit narrowly arrayed for the larger shoe.

While the standard SPa comes with a stock Kent 1600 Ford engine with a single downdraft carburetor, that $995 upgrade in price gets you the same engine balanced, ported and polished with a 100-cc overbore, 9.8:1 pistons, bigger valves, a high-lift cam, reworked Weber 40DCOE carburetors, lightened flywheel, baffled oil sump and polished alloy rocker cover—and 30 additional horsepower.

As built by Yarwood, this is a truly delightful engine. It fires instantly, accelerates without a flat spot or glitch, revs freely to its 6500-rpm redline and pulls with amazing flexibility from almost any speed above idle. You can drive the car in a highly wound state of nervousness or choose to short-shift and torque effortlessly around town, whatever the mood.

Unlike the original Seven, which had a live rear axle, or the Caterham car, which is available with a De Dion setup, the Westfield uses fully independent rear suspension. A Ford Sierra diff is mounted in the frame, with halfshafts going to Westfield-designed alloy hubs located by widely spaced upper and lower A-arms and sprung with coils over Spax adjustable gas-pressurized shocks. Front suspension is also a double A-arm setup, and no anti-roll bars are used at either end.

Ride is remarkably good, for a car of the hair-shirt tradition, and the rear suspension soaks up dips and bumps that would relocate your kidneys in an original Seven. On bumpy corners, however, the rear end can still be induced to chirp and step out slightly, abetted by the basic handling balance of the car, which might be called "catchable oversteer."

In road comfort and wind flow, the Westfield is in all ways the Son of Seven. Wind comes over and around the windshield, drying your eyes, snatching at your hat and roaring in your ears. If you wore a necktie, it would blow straight forward. A set of plexiglass wind wings can eliminate most of this commotion, of course, as do the convertible top and/or side curtains.

The last two items were left with Yarwood, so we did not have the opportunity to try the famous Lotus human jackknife exercise in which one in- and egresses through the windscreen opening, nor can we vouch for

1996 Westfield SPa

MANUFACTURER

Westfield Cars North America
Yarwood Industrial Estate
83485 North Pacific Hwy
Creswell, Ore. 97426

PRICE

List price............................. **$21,000**
Price as tested **$21,995**

    Price as tested includes std equip. (4-wheel disc brakes, lockable luggage box, leather upholstery, all-weather equip.), upgrade package (145-bhp 1700-cc Ford engine; balanced, special pistons, high-lift cam, ported and polished head, twin 40DCOE Webers, lightened flywheel, baffled sump, polished alloy rocker cover) $995.

0–60 mph	**6.1 sec**
0–¼ mi	**14.8 sec**
Top speed	**est 110 mph**
Skidpad	**0.88g**
Slalom	**61.9 mph**
Brake rating..............	**good**

TEST CONDITIONS

Temperature .... 78° F
Wind .... calm
Humidity .... na
Elevation .... 990 ft

SCALE: 10 in. (254mm) DIVISIONS
DRAWING BY BILL DOBSON

ENGINE

Type................ cast-iron block and head, **inline-4**
Valvetrain.................... ohv
Displacement..... 104 cu in./1700 cc
Bore x stroke....... 3.28 x 3.06 in./83.3 x 77.7 mm
Compression ratio 9.8:1
Horsepower
   (SAE)....... **145 bhp @ 5800 rpm**
Bhp/liter 85.3
Torque....... **132 lb-ft @ 4800 rpm**
Maximum engine speed .... 6500 rpm
Fuel delivery..... twin 40DCOE Webers
Fuel..... prem unleaded, 91 pump oct

CHASSIS & BODY

Layout....... **front engine/rear drive**
Body/frame....... tubular steel with alum. panels and composite shell
Brakes
   Front........ **10.0-in. vented discs**
   Rear.............. **9.3-in. discs**
   Assist type................... none
   Total swept area........ 373 sq in.
   Swept area/ton........ 483 sq in.
Wheels .... cast alloy, **14 x 6**
Tires: Avon CR338, **P185/60R-14 82H**
Steering............ **rack & pinion**
   Overall ratio 13.0:1
   Turns, lock to lock........... 2.8
   Turning circle .... 34.1 ft
Suspension
   Front....... **upper & lower A-arms,** coil springs over tube shocks
   Rear........ **upper A-arms, lower reversed A-arms with toe links,** coil springs over tube shocks

DRIVETRAIN

Transmission .... **5-sp manual**

Gear	Ratio	Overall ratio	(Rpm)	Mph
1st	3.31:1	12.98:1	(6500)	32
2nd	1.96:1	7.68:1	(6500)	54
3rd...........	1.36:1	5.33:1	(6500)	78
4th............	1.00:1	3.92:1	(6500)	106
5th............	0.81:1	3.18:1	est (5500)	110

Final drive ratio................................ 3.92:1
Engine rpm @ 60 mph in 5th................. 3000

GENERAL DATA

Curb weight.............. **1405 lb**
Test weight................. 1545 lb
Weight dist (with
   driver), f/r, % 47/53
Wheelbase................. 92.0 in.
Track, f/r .... 49.0 in./49.0 in.
Length.................. **143.0 in.**
Width..................... **62.0 in.**
Height.................... **40.5 in.**
Ground clearance........... 4.0 in.
Trunk space .... 3.0 cu ft

MAINTENANCE

Oil/filter change.... 5000 mi/5000 mi
Tuneup .... 12,000 mi
Basic warranty ..... 12 mo/12,000 mi

ACCOMMODATIONS

Seating capacity 2
Head room .... 34.5 in.
Seat width .... 2 x 16.5 in.
Leg room.................. 44.0 in.
Seatback adjustment........ 20 deg
Seat travel .... 6.0 in.

INTERIOR NOISE

Idle in neutral............. 69 dBA
Maximum in 1st gear .... 103 dBA
Constant 50 mph .... 91 dBA
   70 mph................. 98 dBA

INSTRUMENTATION

150-mph speedometer, 7000-rpm tach, coolant temp, oil temp, fuel level

ACCELERATION

Time to speed	Seconds
0–30 mph	2.2
0–40 mph	3.1
0–50 mph	4.3
0–60 mph	6.1
0–70 mph	8.1
0–80 mph	10.9
0–90 mph	15.3
0–100 mph................	23.8

Time to distance
0–100 ft.................. 2.9
0–500 ft.................. 7.8
0–1320 ft (¼ mi) .. 14.8 @ 89.0 mph

FUEL ECONOMY

Normal driving......... est 26.0 mpg
EPA city/highway ..... est 24/31 mpg
Cruise range .... est 105 miles
Fuel capacity .... 5.0 gal.

BRAKING

Minimum stopping distance
   From 60 mph .... 144 ft
   From 80 mph............. 271 ft
Control .... very good
Pedal effort for 0.5g stop .... na
Fade, effort after six 0.5g stops from
   60 mph .... na
Brake feel............... excellent
Overall brake rating .... good

HANDLING

Lateral accel (200-ft skidpad) ... 0.88g
   Balance .... mild understeer
Speed thru 700-ft slalom.... 61.9 mph
   Balance .... mild understeer
Lateral seat support .... excellent

▼

Test Notes...

■ Down the dragstrip, the Westfield was as easy and forgiving as a car can possibly be. A light, communicative clutch; a snappy shifter; a flexible engine—it relished being pushed hard.

■ Around the skidpad, the SPa was somewhat surprising with its tendency toward oversteer. Bob Yarwood made some adjustments that cured it, although the Westfield's lateral g's didn't improve very much.

■ At first, something felt odd about slaloming the Westfield. And then it became apparent: The loud side exhaust completely obscured the tires' squealing, something normally relied upon to gauge the pace.

Subjective ratings consist of excellent, very good, good, average, poor; na means information is not available.

■ The "eight" in Seight stands for 250 bhp of V-8 thrust somehow snugged into the Westfield engine bay. Whereas the SPa is quick, the Seight is *quicker*. And its dual side pipes mean your fellow passenger can share in your auditory overload.

the weather-tightness of the fabric top, which Yarwood says is excellent. If the top was installed, it would fold down under the locking fiberglass (and only) "trunk" behind the roll-over bar.

Seats in the Westfield are comfortable and supportive (where could you go, anyway?) and have a good range of sliding adjustment, with full shoulder harnesses coming over the top. Instrumentation is complete, but speedometers on both cars had a large margin of optimistic error (Yarwood said this was due to the wrong drive gear being installed on the Seight—the SPa was closer to correct). Neither gas gauge worked, because of a problem with the current VDO senders. With only a 5.0-gallon tank in the SPa and 9.0 in the Seight, you have to keep a sharp eye on the odometer, such as it is.

Gauge problems and the traditional wind flow aside, there are few things to complain about with the SPa. Yarwood's construction quality and attention to detail seem excellent, and the car ran flawlessly though days of hard track testing, commuting in traffic and fast driving in the mountains. It is a delightful car to drive, always fun, and it feels complete, with none of that half-finished rawness you sometimes find in handbuilt cars. Or at least there's no rawness that was not intended in the original design.

And then there's the Seight.

We'll cut right to the chase here. This is a fun hot rod of a car, compromised by two relatively minor problems. First, the overhung pedal assembly seems angled oddly, as though starting halfway through its arc, so clutch and brake-pedal motion feel awkward, as if swinging up and away from your foot.

The only other disappointment is a slight lag in carburetion at tip-in, a sort of one-thousand-one count while the Holley 390-cfm 4-barrel gets its footing and boots fuel and air to the pistons. Yarwood says the carb worked perfectly out of the box, but a carb shop tweaked it during a final tuneup and made it fluffy. (In checking out the problem upon the cars' return, Bob discovered that two vacuum lines had been misrouted.)

But once the engine clears its throat and gets moving, the car rockets down the road with a wonderful roar coming from the two sidepipes, sounding like a pair of 50-caliber machine guns.

The bull in this particular china shop is an all-aluminum 1962-vintage Buick V-8 that started life at 3528 cc but got an 0.040 overbore to 3604. The engine is upgraded with modern Rover V-8 parts—current oil seals, pumps, etc.—and hot-rodded for a bit more thunder. It uses an 0.540-in. lift, 275-degree camshaft especially developed by Crane to take advantage of the Westfield's light weight, as well as an Offenhauser dual-plane intake manifold (soon to be swapped for an Edelbrock), 9.6:1 pistons, a Crane valvetrain kit and an electronic optically fired ignition system. The V-8 is

about 100 lb. heavier than the four, and estimated power output is 250 bhp.

That's a lot of horsepower in a 1630-lb. car, and it does not disappoint. It cannonballs through the quarter mile in 13.8 seconds at 102.0 mph and goes from 0-to-60 mph in just 5.4 sec. That puts it in about the same performance envelope with a Porsche 911 Carrera or Lotus Esprit S4S, in modern terms; and it's about as quick, but not quite as fast in the quarter mile, as a 289 Cobra, to go back a bit. Good company. The Seight is not brutally, insanely fast so that it melts tires or goes inadvertently sideways on the freeway, but the accelerator pedal is definitely connected to the rear tires in a way that causes the driver to grin.

Part of the reason it stays hooked up under power is that it has big tires—Goodyear 205/50-15s at the front and 225/50-15s at the rear (the spare is front only). The car has lots of grip, with handling balance similar to that of the SPa, but without quite the same sense of light and jaunty agility.

Ride, if anything, is slightly better than that of the SPa. On the highway, the Seight feels less jittery and more planted, with compliant, well-damped suspension motion. In 5th gear, cruising at 70–80 mph, it feels relaxed, mellow and profoundly understressed.

More power is available, of course, for those who want to pay for it—a 345-bhp version of the V-8 can be had out of Yarwood's shop.

Regardless of model, Buick V-8 or Ford inline-4, the Westfields are living proof that the laws of physics are unchanging and immutable: Respectable horsepower in a very low, lightweight car always feels good, whether in the Fifties, Sixties or Nineties. ◉

The silent treatment

Type approval has cost the 3.9-litre Westfield SEiGHT its soul-stirring bellow. But it's still a flier, says Andrew Golby

Ready-made SEiGHT looks familiar, but type approval has strangled V8's bellow. Many detail changes have improved car, though, and it's still great fun to drive

Performance hasn't suffered: 0-60mph in 4.3sec

If you've ever been near an original Westfield SEiGHT, you'll remember it. Loud doesn't come close to describing the blood-curdling thunder of its V8 engine.

But it couldn't go on for ever, because the West Midlands-based manufacturer wanted to gain UK low-volume type approval for the 3.9-litre, V8-engined monster. Westfield has put a year and a six-figure sum into the work, and can now sell you a fully built SEiGHT for £25,950. That's £6000 more than the kit version and £3800 more than a Caterham 7 with 2.0-litre Vauxhall power. It's also £4000 less than a Morgan Plus Eight, which uses the same engine, has the same type approval, and has rather less sophisticated underpinnings.

The latest SEiGHT is a very different car from the original we drove five years ago, but the promise of stupendous performance remains. And that means 0-60mph in 4.3sec from the 200bhp pushrod Rover V8, closely related to the one you'll find under the bonnet of a Land Rover Discovery. Torque is a stonking 235lb ft at just 2600rpm, which means huge top-gear flexibility. If you insist, the SEiGHT will carry you all the way from 20mph to 138mph – in fifth.

It has taken Westfield hundreds of hours to get the go-ahead for full SEiGHT production. The company has been over the same hurdles before with its Ford-engined cars, but for a small manufacturer with limited financial means, it's not easy, which is why few kit car makers have managed it.

The most obvious of dozens of changes to the car is the reduction in exhaust noise.

When the man from Westfield fired up the SEiGHT in the factory, I expected thunderous noise to start bouncing off the walls. But it didn't. Type approval has muffled the V8 burble almost completely; it's as simple as that. To pass noise and emissions regulations, Westfield had to fit two three-way catalysts. But we (and Westfield) will be surprised if owners don't ditch the rear silencer soon after purchase, a move which, though not strictly legal, restores much of the legendary V8 thunder.

Once over the aural shock, the changes are less obvious; but there are lots of them. The bonnet, for example, no longer clips on, but is opened using key-locks. They're more fiddly, but more secure. There's extra bodywork to enclose more of the front suspension, and side repeater indicators appear for the first time. Gone are the racing-style wing mirrors, replaced by a pair of Metro-sourced items.

Climbing aboard is an easy exercise for those used to Caterhams. For a start, the exhaust now exits at the rear of the car, not at the side. And the wider body means that, for most, slotting yourself into the cockpit is a doddle. And it's here that the other big change hits you – there's a new dashboard. It looks good and works well, though why you'd have a glovebox without a door in a car as fast as this is a mystery. It is destined to dump its contents in many a lap.

But let's face it, this car is for driving. It's about how fast – and how enjoyably – it can propel you through and between corners. And here comes the next surprise. Although

Brakes effective enough, but don't inspire confidence. Car could teach Caterham lesson in easy access

All-new dash scores highly for looks and practicality, though lidless glovebox daft in fast, open car

the SEiGHT feels very quick, it doesn't quite provide the titanic experience that it promises – for two reasons. First is because, according to the tacho, you have to change up at 5250rpm, and that's where the engine feels strongest. Second is the lack of exhaust noise. The sound is so gagged that your perception of performance is rather numbed. The best measure of how muted the engine really is comes on motorways, where wind noise overtakes the sound of the engine.

But, thanks to a limited slip differential and an excellent gearbox – derived from the MG RV8 – the SEiGHT is easy to drive fast. And all that torque allows you to do it at surprisingly relaxed engine speeds.

Flinging the SEiGHT around a favourite back road is a huge pleasure. It seems well able to handle undulating B-roads at speed without being thrown much off line. And although the 205/50 Goodyear Eagle F1s

can occasionally be unsettled in long, bumpy corners, the car easily recovers its composure. The steering has plenty of feel, but 2.7 turns lock to lock seems a bit under-geared in a car as single-minded as this. Brake feel is less than razor sharp, too. In the toughest spots, you sometimes wonder whether the brakes are quite up to the job, though on paper the all-disc set-up would appear to be sufficient for a 720kg car.

In the end, this Westfield is best described as a mature Seven. Absent is the high-revving, ear-piercing racket. So is the feeling that it has only one object in mind – going absolutely Harry Flatters. You drive this car on torque. It's well beyond the realm of the Morgan Plus Eight in road ability, but has the same long legs. For those who favour a driving experience one peg less intense than an Lotus Elise or a 2.0-litre Caterham, this car fits the bill very well. •

Listen hard and you might hear exhaust. Some owners will blow raspberry at law and lose silencer

FACTFILE

WESTFIELD SEiGHT EURO

HOW MUCH?
Price £25,950
On sale in UK now

HOW FAST?
0-60mph 4.3sec
Top speed 138mph

HOW THIRSTY?
Urban n/a
Extra urban n/a
Combined n/a

HOW BIG?
Length 3702mm (145.7in)
Width 1625mm (64in)
Height 1054mm (41.5in)
Wheelbase 2362mm (93in)
Weight 720kg (1586lb)
Fuel tank 50 litres (11.0 gallons)

ENGINE
Layout 8 cylinders, in vee, 3950cc
Max power 200bhp at 4750rpm
Max torque 235lb ft at 2600rpm
Specific output 51bhp per litre
Power-to-weight ratio 278bhp per tonne
Installation longitudinal, front, rear-wheel drive
Made of aluminium alloy head and block
Bore/stroke 94.04x71mm
Compression ratio 9.35:1
Valve gear 2 per cylinder, sohc
Ignition and fuel electronic fuel injection

GEARBOX
Type 5-speed manual
Ratios/mph per 1000rpm
1st 3.32/7.7
2nd 2.08/12.2
3rd 1.39/18.3
4th 1.10/20.1
5th 0.79/25.5
Final drive ratio 3.38

SUSPENSION
Front double wishbones, coil springs/dampers
Rear double wishbones, coil springs/dampers

STEERING
Type rack and pinion
Lock to lock 2.7

BRAKES
Front 247mm (9.7in) vented discs
Rear 240mm (9.4in) discs
Anti-lock not available

WHEELS AND TYRES
Size 7x15in
Made of aluminium alloy
Tyres 205/50 R15 Goodyear Eagle F1

All manufacturer's figures

ANDY CHRISTODOLO